THE
BOOK OF
FAMILY PRAYER

THE
BOOK OF

FAMILY PRAYER

ROBERT E. WEBBER

HENDRICKSON
PUBLISHERS

THE BOOK OF FAMILY PRAYER
by Robert E. Webber

Hendrickson Publishers, Inc.
P. O. Box 3473
Peabody, Massachusetts 01961-3473

ISBN 1-56563-249-4

Previously published by Thomas Nelson, Inc., Publishers, Nashville, Tennessee.

First printing — May 1996

Printed in the United States of America

In memory
of
my father

The Rev. Chester R. Webber

who passed away while
this book was being born

CONTENTS

PART II

FAMILY READING FOR THE NONFESTIVE TIME OF THE YEAR   223

Following the development of the early church and its literature from A.D. 30 to A.D. 100.

PART III

FAMILY PRAYERS FOR SPECIAL OCCASIONS   273

ACKNOWLEDGMENTS

The art work for the seasons of the Christian year was created by Michael A. Apichella, in conjunction with ancient Christian symbols. The symbol of the family on page 274 is of ancient origin and is used with the permission of Rudolph Koch, *The Book of Signs* (Dover Publications).

INTRODUCTION:
How to Use This Book

For most people Friday evening is a night out on the town, a time to go to a play, party with friends, or simply lounge around at home watching TV and taking it easy. But for an orthodox Jew Friday night is a special night, a religious night, the time to begin *Shabbat,* the Jewish day of rest and religious commemoration.

It was while I was a guest at a *Shabbat* meal service that my own concept of family devotions was challenged and changed. In that context some ancient approaches to family worship were revived for me. My attraction to family worship led me to prepare services for my own family and ultimately to write this book. Let me tell you briefly about my experience.

An Evening to Remember

A number of years ago I became a friend of Rabbi Yechiel Eckstein through the Chicago area evangelical and Jewish dialogue. Yechiel, who is the president of the Holy Land Fellowship and author of the highly acclaimed book, *What Every Christian Should Know about Jews and Judaism,* invited my colleague Morris Inch, myself, and our wives to celebrate *Shabbat* with them.

When Yechiel gave us directions to his home he said, "If you get lost don't call, because we don't answer our phone after sunset on Friday. When we rest, we really rest."

Arriving at the door, Yechiel's lovely wife, Bonnie, enthusiastically greeted us all with an embrace and made us feel at home immediately. As we were taking off our coats, she pointed to a number of candles burning at a side table. "Four of those candles represent our family," she said, "and each of the other four is lighted in honor of your presence." I felt welcome!

After a brief time of friendly conversation, we were invited to sit down at the table. Yechiel sat at one end, Bonnie at the other, the two couples on either side, and the children on both sides of their mother. As I pulled my chair in behind me I wondered what kind of prayer would precede our feast.

"This is a very special meal," Yechiel said, "not only because you are here, but because this meal represents the beginning of our Jewish *Shabbat.* It's a day of rest, a time to remember our Creator and Redeemer, a time to be with the family, a time to establish and deepen our relationships. Some of our table prayers will be said in Hebrew. Just relax and enter the spirit of our thanksgiving."

As Yechiel began speaking in Hebrew to praise God for the fruit of the vine, he took a small loaf of freshly baked bread, broke it, and passed it around the table, bidding us to eat as a sign of our thanks to God. Again, pouring wine into a cup, he lifted it, repeating a Jewish prayer of thanks for the fruit of the vine and, passing it around the table, bade us drink as a sign of our thanks to God. After another prayer our meal began.

As we were eating the delicious food that had been prepared before sundown and kept warm in the oven (no cooking is allowed after sundown), we engaged in a conversation that was more than talk. It was *communication*, communication about our lives, our families, our values, our dreams.

After dessert Yechiel said, "In our tradition we conclude the *Shabbat* meal with more table prayers and psalms. All of this will be done in Hebrew, so simply join in the spirit of what we do." As we all bowed our heads a softly sung litany was begun as Yechiel and Bonnie took turns singing prayers and psalms. Although I could not understand the language, the sense of awe and reverence before the Lord came over me and raised my spirits to the praise of God. After the prayers ended, Yechiel looked at Bonnie and in English spoke of his love for her and of his good fortune in having her as his wife. Then, calling his children to his side, he placed his hands on their heads and, blessing them, sent them happily off to play.

During the meal, on the way home, for weeks afterward, and even to this day, I still frequently reflect on that event. What we were involved in was more than a meal, it was a ritual—a religious ritual—that had *power* to unite a family, recall history, create reverential awe, shape values, and provide a focal point to which memory for both parents and children will return again and again.

Through this experience I was reminded once again that the richness of the Jewish tradition is the heritage of the Christian family. But also, it is a tradition that for many of us has been lost or has fallen into the background. Let me explain.

I do not mean to suggest that most Christian homes don't have prayer at meals or prayers for the children at bedtime or occasional or even regular family prayer. What I mean to say is that most of us do not have table prayers that sanctify time or set apart special occasions and turn them into spiritual festivals that communicate the sense of lifting the event into the very presence of God.

The meal prayers at Rabbi Eckstein's entered us into Sabbath rest. This was no ordinary evening; it was an extraordinary event that turned a meal into a religious experience. But this is only one of many Jewish meal festivals. Others are designed especially for the Passover, for the Day of Atonement, for the Feast of Weeks. And through these meals the cycle of the whole year is lifted up into religious meaning.

As we were driving home that night I remarked to my wife that I wanted to develop meal services for our home that would sanctify time and give special occasions more of a genuine Christian significance. In the next two weeks I wrote feverishly, developing meal services for the seasons of the church year—Advent, Christmas, Epiphany, Lent, Holy Week, Easter, Pentecost—and several services for special occasions like birthdays and anniversaries. This book is an extension and development of these earlier services.

A Book of Family Prayer

The purpose of this book is very basic, even rudimentary. Yet, like most matters of primary importance, its simplicity belies the depth it represents. Let me state the principle first; then I will explain how it works. The principle is this: time, my daily, weekly, and yearly time, is brought into a relationship with Jesus Christ when it is shaped by the experience of His birth, life, death, and resurrection.

Let me explain this principle by stating a fact that we experience every day: the external cycle of time orders our experience. My day is ordered by the rising and setting of the sun; by breakfast, lunch, and dinner; by the act of getting up and going to bed; by the time I must be at work and the time I am free to leave.

In a similar manner my experience of the week is determined by seven days—five to work, one for work around the house, one for worship and rest. Furthermore, my experience of the year is ordered by winter, spring, summer, and fall; by Memorial Day, Fourth of July, Labor Day, Thanksgiving, and the like. I organize my life around these daily, weekly, yearly cycles. They order my life day after day, week after week, year after year. There is no essential change from time to time. I grow older, my children grow up, I change jobs, incidents differ from year to year. But time doesn't change. It's the same cycle, the same order, the same pace.

Now most of us are familiar with ways to sanctify our daily time. We converse with God on getting up and bedding down; we thank Him for our food three times daily, and in special events of the day our thoughts may turn to our Creator and Redeemer. Our week is also sanctified by our Sunday experience, or at least it should be. Sunday celebrates both creation and the re-creation of the world demonstrated in the resurrection. In these ways our daily and weekly time is brought up into Jesus

Christ. The daily ritual of prayer and weekly worship are external rites that order and organize our spiritual experience of time. But what ordering of time organizes our spiritual experience of the year? How can our pilgrimage from year to year be sanctified? That is what *The Family Book of Prayer* is about.

Part I of this book is "Family Prayer for Seasons of the Church Year." After my experience in the home of Rabbi Eckstein I wanted to create services for my family that would order our spiritual experience of time around the most significant event of human history—the earthly life of Jesus Christ. The church year which was developed by our Christian predecessors hundreds of years ago does just that. Consequently these family prayers for Advent, Christmas, Epiphany, Lent, Holy Week, Easter, and Pentecost recall the pilgrimage of Jesus Christ and call us into a yearly cycle spiritually ordered and organized by these events. These services are not merely external rites, but a means of building our personal and family faith in the person of Jesus Christ. The introduction to each of these seasons speaks more specifically to the pattern of spiritual experience that each of these seasons produces.

Part II brings the family through the history of the church and the New Testament records from Pentecost to the end of the first century. Although the church year emphasizes the spread of the church during the months from June through November, I have departed from the lectionary readings to create a weekly family Bible study based on a sequential history of the church drawn mainly from Acts. One unique feature of this study is that the New Testament books are placed in a generally agreed-upon order of their writing according to the Acts narrative. In this way the story of the developing church unfolds from week to week as it actually happened in history. This view of things will revolutionize your understanding of the New Testament, its origin, and meaning.

The final section, Part III, intends to sanctify the special occasions we enjoy in the family: birthdays, anniversaries, Mother's Day, Father's Day, and the like. It emphasizes the spiritual aspects of these occasions and places them in a Christian context.

A few years ago in the Wheaton College chapel, a speaker, who was calling on us to think and respond Christianly to every aspect of life, gave an illustration from an experience he had in South America. He was standing in front of a laundry talking to a South American Roman Catholic when another person ran breathlessly to them declaring that a mutual friend had just died. Upon hearing this the Catholic dropped to his knees, did the sign of the cross, and said a prayer. In the meantime the Wheaton professor responded in surprise and said, "Oh, my goodness, I'm so sorry." After my colleague related the incident he asked the student body, "Which of us expressed a Christian response to the news?"

The point, of course, is clear. Most of us do not have a ready way to truly integrate our faith in Christ into the special events of our lives. Most of us simply say a spontaneous prayer which may or may not be related to the event. While writing this book, my father, to whom this book is dedicated, passed away. I left on the evening of his death to be with my mother. Before I left home, my family gathered at the evening dinner table to pray the service "On the Occasion of a Death." While it was difficult to get through the service because of our love for my father, I felt the prayers and the Scripture readings not only gave comfort to our family, but put death into an entirely Christian perspective. It was a way of celebrating death in light of Christ's resurrection, not as those who have no hope, but in the certainty of life beyond death.

Leading Your Family in Prayer

How are these services best celebrated? In our home we set aside one evening a week to celebrate the meal service. The idea is to make it a special evening with dinner in the dining room, our best dishes and silverware, and good fare. While it is not absolutely necessary, it is preferable when possible to put this family meal service in the context of the Christian season at hand.

It is also helpful to get everyone in the family involved. This service is no monologue; it is dialogic, intended to bring everyone into participation. You can even assign one of the children to take the role of leadership rather than always reserving that role for an adult. Sometimes the service will go quickly, whereas other times lengthy discussions may result. The important thing is to tailor the service to the ages and needs of your family. Do not force a feigned spirituality, simply do it. Do it with sincerity and purposefulness.

Note that most of the prayers are adaptations of Scripture texts. These texts were in most cases the prayers of God's people that arose out of human needs not vastly different from our own. These forebears who struggled with life, with pain and sorrow, with sickness and death, with tragedy and triumph, have given us models of prayer to deal with these circumstances. Similarly, God's saints have left us with the lofty language of praise, adoration,

and thankfulness. Consequently, what we have in these
written texts is a rich spiritual treasury of prayers relating
to every conceivable human situation.

In spite of this scriptural base, some people feel un-
comfortable reading prayers. I come from a tradition, for
example, that spurns written prayers on the ground that
they don't come from the heart. On the other hand,
spontaneous prayer is often criticized as lacking an intel-
ligent correspondence to the situation. What we all want
is prayer that relates to the circumstances, yet is felt
within the heart.

I think there is a way to pray a written prayer that
reaches into the heart. It is to pray it with spiritual intention, just as you sing a written hymn. The value of the
written prayer is that it guides and directs heart and mind
in relation to the situation. For example, before our
Thanksgiving Day meal, we want to pray a prayer of special thanks, but often we cannot find the words to express what is in our hearts. A written prayer of
thanksgiving that represents what God's people feel is a
guide to the heart's desire to offer thanks. Consequently,
when we pray those written words of thanksgiving, in-
tending what the prayer says, the written words guide the
heart's response.

I suggest you approach the written prayers, then, with
the sense that they represent the heartfelt experience of
God's people and that they are words guiding and
expressing your own innermost feelings. Take the liberty
to call for spontaneous prayer during family worship. I
find that just before the dismissal works best.

The prayer services for each season of the church year
include suggestions for an appropriate hymn. I have
listed several titles including traditional hymns, gospel

songs, and in some cases current spirituals and Scripture songs. Let these be prayers. And sing them rather than say them. Since there are spoken prayers in the text already, singing the hymn will provide a different dimension to your prayer. Sound itself captures the mood of the service and creates the sense of prayer you want to achieve. Consider, for example, the sound of Christmas carols and how they actually create the joy they express by the sound of the notes. The sound of the music for each season, whether Advent, Lent, or Easter, assists the inner journey into the spirit and experience of that season. Perhaps it would be a good idea to have a hymn book or two handy.

Remember that you are building in your family a lasting spiritual tradition. Celebrating seasons of the church year as well as special occasions in a prayer context makes a family event extra special. It builds lasting traditions, not only for your family, but for the families of your children.

PART I

Family Prayer for Seasons of the Church Year

ADVENT

ADVENT The circle motif symbolizes wholeness and eternity. The four stylized candles have their origin in the church and have long been associated with the four weeks preceding the nativity. Fire is a symbol of knowledge, and the flames here shine in a dark world with a bright message.

INTRODUCTION TO
Christmastide and Advent

We begin the celebration of the Christian year with
Christmastide, a time that includes the seasons of Advent and Christmas and concludes on the day of Epiphany (which is always celebrated on January 6). The
special nature of Christmastide is captured in a term all
Christians give to it: *The Cycle of Light.*

Christmastide is the cycle of time when the coming of
Christ, as the Light of the World to dispel the darkness
(see John 1:5), is the central and overriding theme of our
worship celebrations. During Advent we wait for the
Light, at Christmas we rejoice in the coming of the great
Light, and on Epiphany we celebrate the manifestation
of the Light beyond the borders of Israel to include even
the Gentiles.

Family devotions during this season include Scripture
and antiphons as well as inquiry and instruction. By
spending time in family worship, the special importance
of what we are celebrating at Christmastide is accentu-
ated.

The word *advent* means "coming." During Advent we

celebrate the coming of Christ at Bethlehem, His coming into our hearts, and His second coming. For four
weeks before Christmas the family devotions are designed to ready us for the coming of our Lord. We begin
at what may seem a distance from the coming of Christ
in Bethlehem and proceed closer each week to the birth.
The family services during the first two weeks emphasize
the second coming of Christ and the need to prepare for
His return.

The preparations we now make for the second coming
of Christ are similar to the preparation Israel was making
for the coming of the Messiah. Terms such as *hope, eager
anticipation, longing,* and *looking toward the day,* all express
the kind of inner feeling Israel had as it waited for the
Messiah. These descriptive terms likewise capture the
feelings we Christians have as we await the consumma-
tion of history and the redemption of all things.

But readiness is more than a feeling. It includes moral
and spiritual preparation, the kind alluded to by Peter
when he wrote, "What manner of persons ought you to
be in holy conduct and godliness?" (2 Pet. 3:11). Consequently, a life of godly conduct is emphasized in the
Scripture readings as well as in the inquiry and instruction of the first two weeks of Advent.

Starting with the third week of Advent, the emphasis
shifts to the feeling of joy. Since the day of His appearing
is coming closer, the accent falls on what Christ will do
in His coming. Both His first and second coming are
related to salvation, redemption, the renewal of creation, the restoration of all things to the Father, and the
sure destruction of evil. Since the putting down of the
devil and his kingdom of darkness makes way for joy,
the sense of that emotion is captured in the Scriptures,

the antiphons, the hymns, prayers, and instruction of the third week.

In the fourth week of Advent we are brought closer to the event of Jesus' birth. Consequently, the accent of our worship falls on the Incarnation: God with us. In this service we are drawn up into the rejoicing of those immediately involved in the events surrounding the miraculous conception of Jesus Christ. We listen to the annunciation to Joseph, the annunciation to Mary, and to Mary's great response, the Magnificat. These readings, together with the prayers and antiphons, bring us closer to Christ and increase our family's anticipation for His birth. (The date of Advent may be found in Appendix I.)

FIRST WEEK OF ADVENT

We Prepare to Worship

Leader: Welcome to the season of Advent, the time dedicated to an eager anticipation of the birth of Jesus. Long, long ago the prophets longed for the birth of Jesus. Isaiah said,
"Now it shall come to pass in the latter days
That the mountain of the LORD's house
Shall be established on the top of the
    mountains,
And shall be exalted above the hills;
And all nations shall flow to it" (2:2).

Now that the time has come, let us heed the words of Isaiah: "Come and let us walk in the light of the LORD" (2:5).

Let us pray.

Father, in this time of anticipation, when we look forward to Your coming in Bethlehem of Judea and to Your coming again in great glory at the end of the age, grant us, O Heavenly

One, grace to shun the power of evil; and clothe us with the light of Your Son, Jesus Christ. May we grow in the light and rise to heavenly life, through Your Son Jesus Christ who lives and reigns with You and the Holy Spirit, one God, now and forever. Amen.

Lighting of the First Advent Candle

As the candle is lighted, read:

"Then the angel said to her, 'Do not be afraid, Mary, for you have found favor with God. And behold, you will conceive in your womb and bring forth a Son, and shall call His name JESUS'" (Luke 1:30–31).

Hymn: *Sing one of the following hymns:*
"Creator of the Stars of Night"
"Angels from the Realms of Glory"
"His Name Is Wonderful"

We Listen to the Word of God

First A reading from Jeremiah:
Reader: "'Behold, the days are coming,' says the LORD, 'that I will perform that good thing which I have promised to the house of Israel and to the house of Judah:
In those days and at that time
I will cause to grow up to David
A Branch of righteousness;
He shall execute judgment and righteousness
  in the earth.
In those days Judah will be saved,

And Jerusalem will dwell safely.
And this is the name by which she will be
    called:
THE LORD
OUR RIGHTEOUSNESS'" (33:14–16).

This is the word of the Lord.

Response: Thanks be to God.

Second   A reading from the gospel of Saint Luke:
Reader: "And there will be signs in the sun, in the
moon, and in the stars; and on the earth dis-
tress of nations, with perplexity, the sea and
the waves roaring; men's hearts failing them
from fear and the expectation of those things
which are coming on the earth, for the powers
of heaven will be shaken. Then they will see
the Son of Man coming in a cloud with power
and great glory. Now when these things begin
to happen, look up and lift up your heads,
because your redemption draws near"
(21:25–28).

This is the word of the Lord.

Response: Thanks be to God.

We Respond to the Word of God

The Inquiry and Instruction

Question: What is the meaning of Advent?

Answer: The word *advent* means "coming." During
Advent we celebrate the coming of Jesus at

31

Bethlehem of Judea into our hearts, and His coming return in judgment.

Question: Why are there four weeks in Advent?

Answer: Each week we prepare for the coming of Christ by celebrating a different theme. This week we enter into a period of "vigilant waiting."

Question: What do we anticipate?

Answer: Christmas is the season of great joy. Advent is the season to prepare for that great joy. In Advent we prepare for the birth of Christ by learning how to wait for the second coming of Christ.

Question: How do we wait?

Answer: Here is what our Lord said about waiting: "Take heed, watch and pray; for you do not know when the time is" (Mark 13:33).

Question: Is there something specific we can do?

Answer: Yes, there is. When we prepare for visitors to come to our home we always clean the house. So it is with Advent. It is a time for spiritual cleaning. Just as the person keeps a clean house for unexpected guests, so we should be constantly obedient to God's will, lest He come when we least expect it.

The Prayers of Intercession

Leader: Let us pray.

Lord, show us Your ways;
Teach us Your paths.
Lead us in Your truth and teach us.
For You are the God of our salvation;
On You we wait all the day.
Remember, O Lord, Your tender mercies and
Your lovingkindnesses,
For they have been from of old.
Do not remember the sins of our youth, nor
our transgressions.
According to Your mercies remember us,
for Your goodness' sake,
O Lord.
Restore us, O God of hosts.
Cause Your face to shine,
and we shall be saved!
(Adapted from Pss. 25 and 80).

Together: Amen.

We Are Sent Forth

Leader: Receive the dismissal.
"'Peace be within your walls,
Prosperity within your palaces.'
For the sake of my brethren and companions
I will now say,
'Peace be within you'" (Ps. 122:7–8).

Together: Thanks be to God.

SECOND WEEK OF ADVENT

We Prepare to Worship

Leader: The theme for the second week of Advent is preparation. Preparation for the coming of our Lord at Christmas, for the coming of the Lord into our hearts, and for the coming of our Lord at the end of history. Hear what Isaiah says to us: "Prepare the way of the LORD;/ Make straight in the desert/A highway for our God" (40:3).

Let us pray.

Father, hasten the day when Your Son of glory will light up the night by his glorious return. Protect us, O Lord, from a preoccupation with the cares of this world. Restrain our selfish greed, and do not withhold from us the joy that fills the hearts of those who love Your Son's appearing. May the darkness of our world not prevent our experiencing the light that You give to those who prepare in faith for Your coming. Hear our prayer, O Lord, through Your Son, our Savior, Jesus Christ, the Lord. Amen.

Lighting of the Second Advent Candle

As the candle is lighted, read:

"Behold, a virgin shall be with child, and bear

a Son, and they shall call His name Immanuel" (Matt. 1:23).

Hymn: *Sing one of the following hymns:*
"Now, Grieving That the Ancient Curse"
"Angels We Have Heard on High"
"O Come, O Come, Emmanuel"

We Listen to the Word of God

First   A reading from Malachi:
Reader: "'Behold, I send My messenger,
              And he will prepare the way before Me.
              And the LORD, whom you seek,
              Will suddenly come to His temple.
              Even the Messenger of the covenant,
              In whom you delight.
              Behold, He is coming,'
              Says the LORD of hosts.
              'But who can endure the day of His coming?
              And who can stand when He appears?
              For He is like a refiner's fire
              And like fuller's soap.
              He will sit as a refiner and a purifier of silver;
              He will purify the sons of Levi,
              And purge them as gold and silver,
              That they may offer to the LORD
              An offering in righteousness'" (3:1–3).

              This is the word of the Lord.

Response: Thanks be to God.

Second   A reading from the gospel of Mark:
Reader: "The beginning of the gospel of Jesus Christ,

35

the Son of God. As it is written in the Prophets: 'Behold, I send My messenger before Your face, who will prepare Your way before You. The voice of one crying in the wilderness: "Prepare the way of the LORD, make His paths straight."' John came baptizing in the wilderness and preaching a baptism of repentance for the remission of sins. And all the land of Judea, and those from Jerusalem, went out to him and were all baptized by him in the Jordan River, confessing their sins. Now John was clothed with camel's hair and with a leather belt around his waist, and he ate locusts and wild honey. And he preached, saying, 'There comes One after me who is mightier than I, whose sandal strap I am not worthy to stoop down and loose. I indeed baptized you with water, but He will baptize you with the Holy Spirit'" (1:1–8).

This is the word of the Lord.

Response: Thanks be to God.

We Respond to the Word of God

The Inquiry and Instruction

Question: How does our spiritual pilgrimage during the second week of Advent differ from the first week of Advent?

Answer: The second week of Advent is very similar to the first. We are to continue preparing for the second coming of our Lord.

36

Question: What does the end of the world have to do with me today?

Answer: Listen again to Saint Peter and he will answer your question: "Therefore, since all these things will be dissolved, what manner of persons ought you to be in holy conduct and godliness?" (2 Pet. 3:11).

Question: What can we do?

Answer: Saint Paul makes four suggestions that we should take to heart: "And this I pray, that your love may abound still more and more in knowledge and all discernment, that you may approve the things that are excellent, that you may be sincere and without offense till the day of Christ, being filled with the fruits of righteousness which are by Jesus Christ, to the glory and praise of God" (Phil. 1:9–11).

The Prayer of Response

Leader: Let us pray.

Father, we bless the name of Jesus.
Let His name endure forever;
May His name continue as long as the sun.
Let us be blessed in Him,
And let all nations call Him blessed.
Restore us, O God of our salvation,
And cause Your anger toward us to cease.
Be not angry with us forever;
Do not prolong Your anger to all generations.
Revive us again, and
Let Your people rejoice in You.

(Adapted from Pss. 72, 85)

We Are Sent Forth

Leader: Receive the dismissal.
"Mercy and truth have met together;
Righteousness and peace have kissed each
other.
Truth shall spring out of the earth,
And righteousness shall look down from
heaven.
Yes, the LORD will give what is good;
And our land will yield its increase.
Righteousness will go before Him,
And shall make His footsteps our pathway"
(Psa. 85:10–13).

Response: Thanks be to God.

THIRD WEEK OF ADVENT.

We Prepare to Worship

Leader: The theme for the third week of Advent is
joy. Let us rejoice, for the birth of Chirst
draws near. For the day is coming when the
Messiah will triumph over evil, and the whole
earth will be renewed.

Let us pray.

Lord, You who will restore all things, may we,
the people of Your family, be filled with joyful
anticipation at the coming of Your Son. Re-

move all sadness that hinders our joy and, like the creation that longs for its redemption, may we joyfully anticipate Your coming now and at the end of the age. We pray through Your Son, Creator and Redeemer of all things. Amen.

Lighting of the Third Advent Candle

As the candle is lighted, read:

"Praise the LORD, call upon His name;
Declare His deeds among the peoples,
Make mention that His name is exalted.
Sing to the LORD,
For He has done excellent things;
This is known in all the earth.
Cry out and shout, O inhabitant of Zion,
For great is the Holy One of Israel in your
    midst!" (Isa. 12:4–6).

Hymn: *Sing one of the following hymns:*
"Behold a Rose from Judah"
"O Come, All Ye Faithful"
"Jesus, Name Above All Names"

We Listen to the Word of God

First   A reading from Zephaniah:
Reader: "Sing, O daughter of Zion!
Shout, O Israel!
Be glad and rejoice with all your heart,
O daughter of Jerusalem!
The LORD has taken away your judgments.
He has cast out your enemy.

The King of Israel, the LORD, is in your
midst;
You shall see disaster no more.
In that day it shall be said to Jerusalem:
'Do not fear;
Zion, let not your hands be weak,
The LORD your God in your midst,
The Mighty One, will save;
He will rejoice over you with gladness,
He will quiet you in His love,
He will rejoice over you with singing'"
(3:14–17).

This is the word of the Lord.

Response: Thanks be to God.

Second A reading from the gospel of John:
Reader: "There was a man sent from God, whose
name was John. This man came for a witness,
to bear witness of the Light, that all through
him might believe. He was not that Light, but
was sent to bear witness of that Light. . . .
Now this is the testimony of John, when the
Jews sent priests and Levites from Jerusalem to
ask him, 'Who are you?' he confessed, and did
not deny, but confessed, 'I am not the Christ.'
And they asked him, 'What then? Are you
Elijah?' He said, 'I am not.' 'Are you the
Prophet?' And he answered, 'No.' Then they
said to him, 'Who are you, that we may give
an answer to those who sent us? What do you
say about yourself?' He said: 'I am "The voice
of one crying in the wilderness: 'Make straight

the way of the LORD'"'" (1:6–8, 19–23).

This is the word of the Lord.

Response: Thanks be to God.

We Respond to the Word of God

The Inquiry and Instruction

Question: Why is the third week of Advent filled with so much joy?

Answer: There are many reasons. One of them is that we are coming closer to the birth of Christ.

Question: What is another reason for joy?

Answer: We rejoice because the Messiah will triumph over evil.

Question: What does that mean?

Answer: "Having disarmed principalities and powers, He made a public spectacle of them, triumphing over them in it" (Col. 2:15).

Question: Is there another reason for joy?

Answer: Yes, because Christ destroys evil we can anticipate a time when justice will rule over the earth. Listen to Isaiah: "Violence shall no longer be heard in your land,/Neither wasting nor destruction within your borders" (60:18).

Question: Is there anything else?

Answer: Yes, the world rejoices because all of creation will be redeemed. Listen to Paul: "The creation itself also will be delivered from the bondage of corruption into the glorious liberty of the children of God" (Rom. 8:21).

Question: What should this mean for us?

Answer: It means we ought to live in the hope of the future. For Paul tells us, "We were saved in this hope" (Rom. 8:24).

The Prayer of Response

Leader: Let us pray.

Lord Jesus Christ, You are coming to bring us salvation. Bring Your salvation to the whole world. Bring Your salvation to this nation. Bring Your salvation to this city. Bring Your salvation to this home.

Response: Amen.

We Are Sent Forth

Leader: Receive the dismissal.
"The LORD opens the eyes of the blind;
The LORD raises those who are bowed down;
The LORD loves the righteous.
The LORD watches over the strangers;
He relieves the fatherless and widow;
But the way of the wicked He turns upside down.
The LORD shall reign forever. . . .
Praise the LORD!" (Ps. 146:8–10).

Response: Thanks be to God.

FOURTH WEEK OF ADVENT

We Prepare to Worship

Leader: This, the fourth week of Advent, is very special; for at this time we celebrate the Incarnation. In the womb of the Virgin Mary, God became one of us, to live among us and teach us, to die for us and save us, to rise again and restore us. Let us, with Mary and Joseph, Elizabeth and Zacharius, rise up and say: "Blessed are you among women, and blessed is the fruit of your womb!" (Luke 1:42).

Let us pray.

Lord, You who created and brought all things into existence, You who redeemed and restored all things fallen, we worship You and we magnify Your holy name. You entered into the womb of the Virgin Mary. You, Creator, became creation. You, Redeemer, became our redemption. We adore You and we bless You, for You became one of us so that we may become one with You. May we whose humanity You share be raised to faith in You. Through Jesus Christ our Lord we pray. Amen.

Lighting of the Fourth Advent Candle

As the candle is lighted, say the Magnificat:

"My soul magnifies the Lord,/And my spirit has rejoiced in God my Savior" (Luke 1:47).

Hymn: *Sing one of the following hymns:*
"O Come, O Come, Emmanuel"
"Hark! The Herald Angels Sing"

We Listen to the Word of God

First Reader: A reading from the annunciation to Joseph: "Now the birth of Jesus Christ was as follows: After His mother Mary was betrothed to Joseph, before they came together, she was found with child of the Holy Spirit. Then Joseph her husband, being a just man, and not wanting to make her a public example, was minded to put her away secretly. But while he thought about these things, behold, an angel of the Lord appeared to him in a dream, saying, 'Joseph, son of David, do not be afraid to take to you Mary your wife, for that which is conceived in her is of the Holy Spirit. And she will bring forth a Son, and you shall call His name JESUS, for He will save His people from their sins'" (Matt. 1:18–21).

This is the word of the Lord.

Response: Thanks be to God.

Second Reader: A reading from the annunciation to Mary: "Now in the sixth month the angel Gabriel was sent by God to a city of Galilee named Nazareth, to a virgin betrothed to a man whose name was Joseph, of the house of David. The virgin's name was Mary. And having come in, the angel said to her. 'Rejoice, highly favored one, the Lord is with you;

blessed are you among women!' But when she saw him, she was troubled at his saying, and considered what manner of greeting this was. Then the angel said to her, 'Do not be afraid, Mary, for you have found favor with God. And behold, you will conceive in your womb and bring forth a Son, and shall call His name JESUS. He will be great, and will be called the Son of the Highest; and the Lord God will give Him the throne of His father David. And He will reign over the house of Jacob forever, and of His kingdom there will be no end.' Then Mary said to the angel, 'How can this be, since I do not know a man?' And the angel answered and said to her, 'The Holy Spirit will come upon you, and the power of the Highest will overshadow you; therefore, also, that Holy One who is to be born will be called the Son of God. Now indeed, Elizabeth your relative has also conceived a son in her old age; and this is now the sixth month for her who was called barren. For with God nothing will be impossible.' Then Mary said, 'Behold the maidservant of the Lord! Let it be to me according to your word.' And the angel departed from her" (Luke 1:26–38).

This is the word of the Lord.

Response: Thanks be to God.

We Respond to the Word of God

Question: Why is the fourth Sunday of Advent so special?

Answer: Because we emphasize the Incarnation of God in the womb of the Virgin Mary.

Question: What is the Incarnation?

Answer: The word means "to enflesh." In the Incarnation, God the Son became one of us in the womb of the Virgin Mary.

Question: Why is this so important?

Answer: Because God's becoming man was necessary for our salvation.

Question: What does the Bible teach us about the Incarnation?

Answer: The Incarnation is the fulfillment of prophecy given to David. "When your days are fulfilled and you rest with your fathers, I will set up your seed after you, who will come from your body, and I will establish . . . the throne of his kingdom forever" (2 Sam. 7:12–13).

The Incarnation also fulfills a prophecy given to Isaiah. "Therefore the Lord Himself will give you a sign: Behold, the virgin shall conceive and bear a Son, and shall call His name Immanuel" (7:14).

And the Incarnation also fulfills a prophecy given to Micah.
"But you, Bethlehem Ephrathah,
Though you are little among the
    thousands of Judah,
Yet out of you shall come forth to Me
The One to be ruler in Israel,

Whose goings forth have been from
   of old,
From everlasting" (5:2).

Question: Why are the prophecies so important?

Answer: Matthew answers that question. "And she will bring forth a Son, and you shall call His name JESUS, for He will save His people from their sins" (1:21).

Question: What should we do?

Answer: Paul describes the appropriate response: "If you confess with your mouth the Lord Jesus and believe in your heart that God has raised Him from the dead, you will be saved" (Rom. 10:9).

The Prayer of Response

Leader: Let us pray.

Let the heavens praise Your wonders, O Lord,
For who in the heavens can be compared to
   the Lord?
Who is mighty like You, O Lord?
The heavens are Yours, the earth also is Yours;
The world and all its fullness,
   You have founded them.
You have a mighty arm, and Your hand is
   strong.
Mercy and truth go before You,
And in Your righteousness we are exalted.
Lord, may we walk in Your countenance,
May we rejoice in Your name,

May we love righteousness,
For You are our shield.
You are our king,
The Holy One, in whose name we pray,
Amen.

(Adapted from Ps. 89.)

We Are Sent Forth

Leader: Receive the dismissal.

"Now to Him who is able to establish you according to my gospel and the preaching of Jesus Christ, according to the revelation of the mystery which was kept secret since the world began but now has been made manifest, and by the prophetic Scriptures has been made known to all nations, according to the commandment of the everlasting God, for obedience to the faith—to God, alone wise, be glory through Jesus Christ forever. Amen" (Rom. 16:25–27).

Response: Thanks be to God.

CHRISTMAS AND EPIPHANY

CHRISTMAS The six-sided star calls to the worshiper's mind the Hebrew star of David, the line from which Christ emerged. Since the late Roman era, the star of Bethlehem has been used as a typical symbol of Christ's birth. The idea arises from the gospel account of the star that guided the Magi.

INTRODUCTION TO
Christmas and Epiphany

We now enter into the Christmas season itself! After
Advent, the long period of preparation, we now burst
forth into Christmas singing carols and celebrating to-
gether the birth of our Lord, the Savior of the world. For
Christmas there are four family services: Christmas Eve,
Christmas Day, the first week after Christmas, and
Epiphany.

The emphasis on Christmas Eve is on *anticipation.* The
reading of the genealogy of Jesus from Matthew, a passage that is seldom read in our churches, let alone our
homes, emphasizes the element of waiting. This is the
night when we look for "the blessed hope and glorious
appearing of our great God and Savior Jesus Christ"
(Titus 2:13). In this single verse the double theme of
Advent—waiting for the birth and waiting for the second coming—is brought together.

The emphasis on Christmas Day is on encounter. On
this great day, the feast of our Lord's birth, we are
encountered by the presence of God among us; and we
join with the angels to sing, "Glory to God in the high-

est,/And on earth peace, good will toward men!" (Luke 2:14).

In this great encounter we see the glory of God. "The word became flesh and dwelt among us, and we beheld His glory, the glory as of the only begotten of the Father, full of grace and truth" (John 1:14).

Since Christmas season lasts for twelve days, from December 25 to January 6, one more service has been added. This service, which emphasizes Jesus' family, is to be celebrated the week after Christmas, sometime before Epiphany on January 6. Not much is written about Jesus between His birth and ministry. However, what has been written and recorded in Scripture about the boyhood of Jesus always places Him in the context of His holy family. Consequently, this service points to the commitment and love within the family of Jesus as an example for our own families.

Christmastide ends on January 6 with the celebration of Epiphany. The word *epiphany* means "manifestation" and refers to the beginning of Christ's public ministry. This is symbolized by the coming of the Magi, Gentiles who fell at the feet of Jesus, manifested to them by a star. The service not only emphasizes the worship of the Magi, a love that we are to emulate, but points as well to a hidden prophecy within this event, namely, the extension of the Messiah's kingdom beyond Israel to include all people. By ending Christmastide with the feast of Epiphany, we anticipate the ministry of Jesus through the church to the whole world, a ministry we will celebrate in our home services during the weeks of Epiphany.

As you celebrate these services with your family, note the progression that moves toward the birth of Christ and the expansion that moves beyond His birth to the whole world, awaiting the redemption of all things at the end of time. Think in terms of an hourglass set on its side. As Christians, we begin at the center, Christ's birth, and then let the message of Christ extend over the whole earth. In this way, the spiritual pilgrimage you make as a family will join with the pilgrimage of Christians around the world who celebrate the coming of the Messiah, Jesus Christ.

A favorite symbol to use during the Christmas season is the Christ candle. This candle, which signifies the Light from the root of Jesse, is placed in the center of the Advent wreath and lighted along with the Advent candles at the celebration of each of these services.

CHRISTMAS EVE

We Prepare to Worship

Leader: The day we have been longing for is coming near. Tonight we are filled with anticipation as we wait in expectancy with eagerness for the coming of Jesus, the babe born in Bethlehem.

Let us pray.

Father, we have waited for this time, watching, praying, and preparing. Grant, as we wait these final hours, that we may sleep in peace and awake in the joy of Your Son's appearing. We pray these words through Jesus. Amen.

Lighting of the Advent Candles

As the candles are lighted, say:
"The people who have walked in darkness have seen a great light" (Isa. 9:2).

Hymn: *Sing one of the following hymns:*
"Silent Night, Holy Night"
"What Child Is This?"

We Listen to the Word of God

First   A reading from Isaiah:
Reader: "For Zion's sake I will not hold My peace,
And for Jerusalem's sake I will not rest,
Until her righteousness goes forth as bright-
    ness,
And her salvation as a lamp that burns.
The Gentiles shall see your righteousness,
And all kings your glory.
You shall be called by a new name,
Which the mouth of the LORD will name.
You shall also be a crown of glory
In the hand of the LORD,
And a royal diadem
In the hand of your God.
You shall no longer be termed
    Forsaken,
Nor shall your land any more be termed
    Desolate;
But you shall be called Hephzibah, and your
    land Beulah,
For the LORD delights in you,
And your land shall be married.
For as a young man marries a virgin,
So shall your sons marry you;
And as the bridegroom rejoices over the
    bride,
So shall your God rejoice over you"
    (62:1–5).

This is the word of the Lord.

Response: Thanks be to God.

Second
Reader: A reading from Matthew:

"The book of the genealogy of Jesus Christ, the Son of David, the Son of Abraham: Abraham begot Isaac, Isaac begot Jacob, and Jacob begot Judah and his brothers. Judah begot Perez and Zerah by Tamar, Perez begot Hezron, and Hezron begot Ram. Ram begot Amminadab, Amminadab begot Nahshon, and Nahshon begot Salmon. Salmon begot Boaz by Rahab, Boaz begot Obed by Ruth, Obed begot Jesse, and Jesse begot David the king. David the king begot Solomon by her who had been the wife of Uriah. Solomon begot Rehoboam, Rehoboam begot Abijah, and Abijah begot Asa. Asa begot Jehoshaphat, Jehoshaphat begot Joram, and Joram begot Uzziah. Uzziah begot Jotham, Jotham begot Ahaz, and Ahaz begot Hezekiah. Hezekiah begot Manasseh, Manasseh begot Amon, and Amon begot Josiah. Josiah begot Jeconiah and his brothers about the time they were carried away to Babylon. And after they were brought to Babylon, Jeconiah begot Shealtiel, and Shealtiel begot Zerubbabel. Zerubbabel begot Abiud, Abiud begot Eliakim, and Eliakim begot Azor. Azor begot Zadok, Zadok begot Achim, and Achim begot Eliud. Eliud begot Eleazar, Eleazar begot Matthan, and Matthan begot Jacob. And Jacob begot Joseph the husband of Mary, of whom was born Jesus who is called Christ. So all the generations from Abraham to David are fourteen generations, from David until the captivity in Babylon are fourteen generations, and from the captivity in Babylon until the Christ are fourteen generations" (1:1–17).

This is the word of the Lord.

Response: Thanks be to God.

We Respond to the Word of God

The Inquiry and Instruction

Question: Why is this night so important to us?

Answer: Because it brings us close to the compassion and grace of our Lord.

Question: What does Christmas have to do with God's compassion?

Answer: Paul refers to the coming of Jesus as an expression of God's compassion toward us: "When the kindness and love of God our Savior toward men appeared" (Titus 3:4).

Question: Does grace appear to us tonight as well?

Answer: Yes. In reference to Christ, Paul wrote, "The grace of God that brings salvation has appeared to all men" (Titus 2:11).

The Prayer of Response

Leader: Let us pray.

"You spoke in a vision to Your holy one,
And said: 'I have given help to one who is
        mighty;
I have exalted one chosen from the people.

I have found My servant David;
With My holy oil I have anointed him,
With whom My hand shall be established;
Also My arm shall strengthen him. . . .
He shall cry to Me, "You are my Father,
My God, and the rock of my salvation."
Also I will make him My firstborn,
The highest of the kings of the earth.
My mercy I will keep for him forever,
And My covenant shall stand firm with him.
His seed also I will make to endure forever,
And his throne as the days of heaven' "
    (Ps. 89:19–21, 26–29).

Lord, for this and all Your gifts, we give You thanks.

We Are Sent Forth

Leader: Receive the dismissal.
This is the night when we look "for the blessed hope and glorious appearing of our great God and Savior Jesus Christ" (Titus 2:13).

Response: Thanks be to God.

CHRISTMAS DAY

We Prepare to Worship

Leader: The day we have been looking for has come. Today we celebrate the birth of Christ, God's encounter with the world and with us. Long, long ago Isaiah said:
"The glory of the LORD shall be revealed,
And all flesh shall see it together;
For the mouth of the LORD has spoken" (40:5).

Today we celebrate the fulfillment of that prophecy. Alleluia!

Let us pray.

Father, we have kept vigil waiting for Your Son, and the dawning of salvation. Now that the day of birth and salvation has come, fill our hearts with gratitude; center our thoughts on the Babe in the manger; let our words be in praise of Thee and teach us to walk after His example. Through Jesus Christ our Lord who lives and reigns with You and the Holy Spirit forever. Amen.

Lighting of the Christmas Candles

As the candles are lighted, say:

"Glory to God in the highest,
And on earth peace, good will toward men!"
(Luke 2:14).

Hymn: *Sing one of the following hymns:*
"O Come, All Ye Faithful"
"There's a Song in the Air"

We Listen to the Word of God

First A reading from Isaiah:
Reader: "The people who walked in darkness
Have seen a great light;
Those who dwelt in the land of the shadow of
  death,
Upon them a light has shined. . . .
For unto us a Child is born,
Unto us a Son is given;
And the government will be upon His
  shoulder.
And His name will be called
Wonderful, Counselor, Mighty God,
Everlasting Father, Prince of Peace.
Of the increase of His government and peace
There will be no end.
Upon the throne of David and over His
  kingdom,
To order it and establish it with judgment and
  justice
From that time forward, even forever.
The zeal of the LORD of hosts will perform this"
  (9:2–7).

This is the word of the Lord.

Response: Thanks be to God.

Second A reading from the gospel according to John:
Reader: "In the beginning was the Word, and the

Word was with God, and the Word was God. He was in the beginning with God. All things were made through Him, and without Him nothing was made that was made. In Him was life, and the life was the light of men. And the light shines in the darkness, and the darkness did not comprehend it. There was a man sent from God, whose name was John. This man came for a witness, to bear witness of the Light, that all through him might believe. He was not that Light, but was sent to bear witness of that Light. That was the true Light which gives light to every man who comes into the world. He was in the world, and the world was made through Him, and the world did not know Him. He came to His own, and His own did not receive Him. But as many as received Him, to them He gave the right to become children of God, even to those who believe in His name: who were born, not of blood, nor of the will of the flesh, nor of the will of man, but of God. And the Word became flesh and dwelt among us, and we beheld His glory, the glory as of the only begotten of the Father, full of grace and truth" (1:1–14).

We Respond to the Word of God

The Inquiry and Instruction

Question: The wonder of Christmas can be set in three paradoxes that meet us on this glorious day. What is a paradox?

Answer: It is a seeming contradiction because it contains two sides of the same thing.

Question: What are they?

Answer: First is the paradox of the invisible and the visible. The Bible teaches us that God is a spirit. He cannot be seen or touched. Yet, in the birth of Christ, God is made visible. Isaiah says, "The glory of the LORD shall be revealed" (40:5). And Saint John writes, "We beheld His glory" (1:14).

Question: What is the second paradox?

Answer: Jesus is both King and Servant. The psalmist tells us, "I have set My King/On My holy hill" (Ps. 2:6). Yet Paul tells us that in His birth He took "the form of a servant. . . . He humbled Himself and became obedient to the point of death" (Phil. 2:7–8).

Question: And is there a third?

Answer: Yes, the contrast between His glory and the place of His birth. Saint John tells us, "We beheld His glory" (1:14); yet Luke tells us that the shepherds came and found the "Babe lying in a manger" (2:16).

Question: What are we to make of this?

Answer: God became one of us in order that we might be brought to Him. "Glory to God in the highest,/And on earth peace, good will toward men!" (Luke 2:14).

The Prayer of Response

Leader: Let us pray.

Lord, we sing to You a new song,
We bless Your name,
And we proclaim the good news of Your
   salvation.
O Lord, You are great and greatly to be
   praised;
Honor and majesty belong to You;
Strength and beauty are Yours.
Lord, let the heavens rejoice and let the earth
   be glad;
Let the sea roar, and all its fullness;
Let the field be joyful, and all that is in it.
For You have come,
You have come to save us,
And You will come to judge the earth.
You will judge the world with righteousness.
And the peoples with truth. Alleluia! Amen.
                    (Adaptation of Ps. 96)

We Are Sent Forth

Leader: Receive the dismissal.
"You who love the LORD, hate evil!
He preserves the souls of His saints;
He delivers them out of the hand of the
   wicked.
Light is sown for the righteous,
And gladness for the upright in heart.
Rejoice in the LORD, you righteous,
And give thanks at the remembrance of His
   holy name" (Ps. 97:10–12).

Response: Thanks be to God.

FIRST WEEK AFTER CHRISTMAS

We Prepare to Worship

Leader: It has been a custom in the church for many years to celebrate the presence of our Lord in a family. Mary, Joseph, and Jesus have left us an example to follow, a family of people committed to each other and to the will of God.

Let us pray.

Father, You, who know what it means to live in community and to have a Son whom You love, grant us, through Your Son's earthly family, to gain a vision of family love and so to live after the example of the Holy Family, that Your love may be seen in our relationships. Grant us this request, O Heavenly One, through Your Son, our example. Amen.

Lighting of the Advent and Christmas Candles.

Say the following:

"And Jesus increased in wisdom and stature, and in favor with God and men" (Luke 2:52).

Hymn: *Sing one of the following hymns:*
"A Child Is Born in Bethlehem"
"What Child Is This?"

We Listen to the Word of God

**First
Reader:** A reading from the Letter to the Colossians: "Therefore, as the elect of God, holy and beloved, put on tender mercies, kindness, humbleness of mind, meekness, longsuffering; bearing with one another, and forgiving one another, if anyone has a complaint against another; even as Christ forgave you, so you also must do. But above all these things put on love, which is the bond of perfection. And let the peace of God rule in your hearts, to which also you were called in one body; and be thankful. Let the word of Christ dwell in you richly in all wisdom, teaching and admonishing one another in psalms and hymns and spiritual songs, singing with grace in your hearts to the Lord. And whatever you do in word or deed, do all in the name of the Lord Jesus, giving thanks to God the Father through Him" (3:12–17).

This is the word of the Lord.

Response: Thanks be to God.

**Second
Reader:** A reading from the gospel of Luke: "And the Child grew and became strong in spirit, filled with wisdom; and the grace of God was upon Him. His parents went to Jerusalem every year at the Feast of the Passover. And when He was twelve years old, they went up to Jerusalem according to the custom of the feast. When they had finished the days, as they returned, the Boy Jesus lingered be-

hind in Jerusalem. And Joseph and His mother did not know it; but supposing Him to have been in the company, they went a day's journey, and sought Him among their relatives and acquaintances. So when they did not find Him, they returned to Jerusalem, seeking Him. Now so it was that after three days they found Him in the temple, sitting in the midst of the teachers, both listening to them and asking them questions. And all who heard Him were astonished at His understanding and answers. So when they saw Him, they were amazed; and His mother said to Him, 'Son, why have You done this to us? Look, Your father and I have sought You anxiously.' And He said to them, 'Why is it that you sought Me? Did you not know that I must be about My Father's business?' But they did not understand the statement which He spoke to them. Then He went down with them and came to Nazareth, and was subject to them, but His mother kept all these things in her heart. And Jesus increased in wisdom and stature, and in favor with God and men" (2:40–52).

This is the word of the Lord.

Response: Thanks be to God.

We Respond to the Word of God

The Inquiry and Instruction

Question: Why does the gospel reading tell us that Jesus was subject to his parents?

Answer: Because subjection to one another is a key element in a happy family.

Question: What does that mean?

Answer: It means we each look out for the other person and put the needs of others above our own.

Question: Does the Bible teach that elsewhere?

Answer: Yes, listen to Paul's teaching: "Wives, submit to your own husbands, as is fitting in the Lord. Husbands, love your wives and do not be bitter toward them. Children, obey your parents in all things, for this is well pleasing to the Lord. Fathers, do not provoke your children, lest they become discouraged. Servants, obey in all things your masters according to the flesh, not with eyeservice, as menpleasers, but in sincerity of heart, fearing God. And whatever you do, do it heartily, as to the Lord and not to men" (Col. 3:18–23).

The Prayer of Response

Leader: Let us pray.

Lord, may this family fear You and walk in Your ways.
When we eat the labor of our hands,
May we also be happy and may it be well with us.
Let the wife of this house be like a fruitful vine,
And the children like olive plants.
Let the man of this house and all of us fear You and be blessed.

Lord, bless all the days of our lives;
And may we see our children's children,
We pray, through Jesus Christ our Lord.
Amen.

(Adapted from Ps. 128)

We Are Sent Forth

Leader: Receive the dismissal.
"The LORD bless you out of Zion,
And may you see the good of Jerusalem
All the days of your life.
Yes, may you see your children's children"
(Ps. 128:5–6).

Response: Thanks be to God.

EPIPHANY (JANUARY 6)

We Prepare to Worship God

Leader: Many centuries ago three wise men made a long trip to Bethlehem, to worship and adore the Christ Child. Today, we celebrate their journey, and with them we bow in humble adoration to extol the Babe of Bethlehem.

Let us pray.

Father, You who brought the Magi to the feet of Jesus, bring us, Your servants, to His manger. May we with the nations adore Him. Reveal Him to us as the Word made flesh, kindle

within us the light of His countenance, and
inflame our hearts with His love. We ask this
through our Lord Jesus Christ, Your Son, who
lives and reigns with You and the Holy Spirit,
one God, forever and ever. Amen.

Hymn: *Sing one of the following hymns:*
"As with Gladness Men of Old"
"We Three Kings of Orient Are"

We Listen to the Word of God

First   A reading from Isaiah:
Reader: "Arise, shine;
For your light has come!
And the glory of the LORD is risen upon you.
For behold, the darkness shall cover the
     earth,
And deep darkness the people;
But the LORD will arise over you,
And His glory will be seen upon you.
The Gentiles shall come to your light,
And kings to the brightness of your rising.
'Lift up your eyes all around, and see:
They all gather together, they come to you;
Your sons shall come from afar,
And your daughters shall be nursed at your
     side.
Then you shall see and become radiant,
And your heart shall swell with joy;
Because the abundance of the sea shall be
     turned to you,
The wealth of the Gentiles shall come to you.
The multitude of camels shall cover your land,

The dromedaries of Midian and Ephah;
All those from Sheba shall come;
They shall bring gold and incense,
And they shall proclaim the praises of the
    LORD'" (60:1–6).

This is the word of the Lord.

Response: Thanks be to God.

Second   A reading from the gospel of Matthew:
Reader: "Now after Jesus was born in Bethlehem of
Judea in the days of Herod the king, behold,
wise men from the East came to Jerusalem,
saying, 'Where is He who has been born King
of the Jews? For we have seen His star in the
East and have come to worship Him.' When
Herod the king heard these things, he was
troubled, and all Jerusalem with him. And
when he had gathered all the chief priests and
scribes of the people together, he inquired of
them where the Christ was to be born. So
they said to him, 'In Bethlehem of Judea, for
thus it is written by the prophet:
"But you, Bethlehem, in the land of Judah;
Are not the least among the rulers of Judah;
For out of you shall come a Ruler
Who will shepherd My people Israel."'
Then Herod, when he had secretly called the
wise men, determined from them what time
the star appeared. And he sent them to Bethlehem and said, 'Go and search diligently for
the young Child, and when you have found
Him, bring back word to me, that I may come

and worship Him also.' When they heard the king, they departed; and behold, the star which they had seen in the East went before them, till it came and stood over where the young Child was. When they saw the star, they rejoiced with exceedingly great joy. And when they had come into the house, they saw the young Child with Mary His mother, and fell down and worshiped Him. And when they had opened their treasures, they presented gifts to Him: gold, frankincense, and myrrh. Then, being divinely warned in a dream that they should not return to Herod, they departed for their own country another way" (2:1–12).

This is the word of the Lord.

Response: Thanks be to God.

We Respond to the Word of God

The Inquiry and Instruction

Question: Is there a meaning behind the story of the Magi?

Answer: It contains some very significant meanings for the past, the present, and the future.

Question: What is its past meaning?

Answer: It is the sign that Christ is not only for the Jews but also for the Gentiles. Paul speaks of this truth in his letter to the Ephesians: "By revelation He made known to me the mystery . . . which in other ages was not made known . . . that the Gentiles should be fellow heirs . . . partakers of His promise in Christ" (3:3–6).

Question: What is the future meaning?

Answer: Its future meaning will be experienced at the end of the world. The central theme of Matthew's account is the manifestation of the Lord's glory to all peoples. This vision will be fulfilled in the age to come.

Question: What is the future meaning?

Answer: What will occur in the future we are to make present now. We are to fall before Christ and adore Him as the savior of the world.

The Prayer of Response

Leader: Let us, like the Magi, kneel down and pray.
O God, may You have dominion from sea to sea.
Let all the kings fall down before You and all nations serve Your holy name.
Spare the poor and the needy and redeem their lives from oppression and violence.
Let there be abundance of grain on the earth,
And let Your people flourish like the grass of the earth.
Let Your name endure forever,
And may all nations call Your Son blessed.
(Adaptation of Ps. 72)

We Are Sent Forth

Leader: Receive the dismissal.
"Blessed be the LORD God, the God of Israel,
Who only does wondrous things!
And blessed be His glorious name forever!
And let the whole earth be filled with His
glory" (Ps. 72:18–19).

Response: Thanks be to God.

ORDINARY TIME

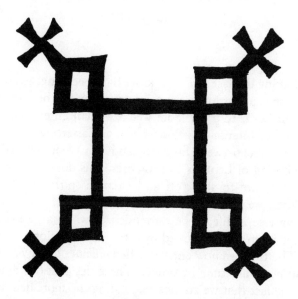

EPIPHANY   The motif here suggests a manifestation of Christ's divine nature, especially to the nations (Gentiles) by the use of the number four and the ancient symbol, the cross. The ancients thought of the world as having four corners; therefore, the Christian message is revealed to the entire world.

INTRODUCTION TO
Ordinary Time

During the last seven weeks we have been engaged in a very special but intense time of preparing for the coming of our Lord. In a few more weeks we will enter another period of intense devotion known as Eastertide.

The time between Epiphany and Ash Wednesday (the beginning of Lent) is less intense. This does not mean that we are to slack off and become spiritually lazy. Rather, we recognize that spiritual discipline, like everything else in life, is best attended to when a period of great intensity is followed by a time of variation.

The time we now enter is called *ordinary time* by some and *nonfestive* time by others. These designations point to the fact that we are not celebrating the more decisive moments in the life of Christ, as we do at Christmastide or Eastertide.

Nevertheless, what we concentrate on in our devotions during Epiphany is certainly not unimportant! Indeed not. We follow Jesus in the beginning of His public ministry and listen attentively to what He has to teach us. We go with Him into Galilee, follow Him as He calls

His disciples, and listen attentively to His teaching, particularly the Sermon on the Mount.

The message of the nine possible celebrations between Epiphany and Lent call us into discipleship. The first celebration takes us to the baptism of our Lord, to the public recognition of His role as Messiah and the beginning of His adult ministry. In the second week we hear John declare, "Behold! The Lamb of God who takes away the sin of the world!" (1:29). There is to be no doubt that His mission of salvation has begun and that He and no other has been sent to accomplish the hope of Israel. In the third week we go with Jesus to Galilee, where He calls His disciples to follow Him, and like them we too drop our nets and follow.

Then in the fourth through the eighth week we attend to the Sermon on the Mount. Jesus speaks to us of the poor (fourth week), of our calling to be salt and light (fifth week), of our need to choose to live by love (sixth week), to apply love to our neighbors and even our enemies (seventh week), and to rest on the providential care of God (eighth week).

The final week before Lent and the beginning of a penitential season is the vision of Christ's glory with the Father in the Transfiguration. All the readings after Epiphany have brought us closer to Jesus; now, before He begins to suffer, we see Him for who He really is—the one united to the Father, the Messiah, the Son of God.

It should be noted that the length of time between Epiphany and Lent will vary according to the date of Easter. There can be as few as five weeks and as many as nine between Epiphany and Lent. In order to determine how many weeks you will celebrate ordinary time after Epiphany, check the chart in Appendix I, then choose which of the family services you will use. It is always a good idea to include the baptism at the beginning and the Transfiguration at the end. This way your family will be taken from the voice at the baptism to the voice at the Transfiguration and experience indeed that "This is My beloved Son, in whom I am well pleased. Hear Him!" (Matt. 3:17; 17:5).

Further, in keeping with a time that is ordinary and nonfestive as opposed to *extra*ordinary and festive, the services are shorter. Specifically the antiphons, along with the inquiry and instruction, have been dropped as a way of expressing the change of atmosphere in the Epiphany season at Eastertide. In the meantime let your family relax and concentrate on the teachings of Jesus as a preparation for the intense period of spiritual renewal that will come during Lent.

FIRST WEEK AFTER EPIPHANY

The Call to Worship

Leader: The theme of our devotion is the baptism of Jesus.

Hear the word of the Lord: "Behold! My Servant whom I uphold, / My Elect One in whom My soul delights! / I have put My Spirit upon Him" (Isa. 42:1).

Let us pray.

Father, as Your Son Jesus Christ became Your servant and obediently carried out Your will, so grant us a portion of Your Spirit, that we may do Your will, through Jesus Christ our Lord. Amen.

The Scripture Readings

First Reader: A Reading from Isaiah:

"Behold! My Servant whom I uphold,
My Elect One in whom My soul delights!
I have put My Spirit upon Him;
He will bring forth justice to the Gentiles.

He will not cry out, nor raise His voice,
Nor cause His voice to be heard in the street.
A bruised reed He will not break,
And smoking flax He will not quench;
He will bring forth justice for truth.
He will not fail nor be discouraged. . . .
Thus says God the LORD,
Who created the heavens and stretched them
     out,
Who spread forth the earth and that which
     comes from it,
Who gives breath to the people on it,
And spirit to those who walk on it:
'I, the LORD, have called You in
     righteousness,
And will hold Your hand;
I will keep You and give You as a covenant to
     the people,
As a light to the Gentiles,
To open blind eyes,
To bring out prisoners from the prison,
Those who sit in darkness from the prison
     house'" (42:1–7).

This is the word of the Lord.

Response: Thanks be to God.

Second Reader: A reading from the gospel of Matthew: "Then Jesus came from Galilee to John at the Jordan to be baptized by him. And John tried to prevent Him, saying, 'I have need to be baptized by You, and are You coming to me?' But Jesus answered and said to him, 'Permit it to be so now, for thus it is fitting for us to fulfill all righteousness.' Then he allowed Him. Then Jesus, when He had been baptized, came up immediately from the water; and behold, the heavens were opened to Him, and He saw the Spirit of God descending like a dove and alighting upon Him. And suddenly a voice came from heaven, saying, 'This is My beloved Son, in whom I am well pleased'" (3:13–17).

This is the word of the Lord.

Response: Thanks be to God.

Hymn: *Sing one of the following hymns:*
"Come, Holy Spirit, Dove Divine"
"Breathe on Me, Breath of God"

Leader: Let us pray.

Lord, we confess that the throne of
Your Son is forever and ever.
He loves righteousness and hates wickedness.
You have anointed Him, O Lord,
With the oil of gladness;
His garments are scented with myrrh.
O Lord, grant that we who have been baptized
    into His name
May live in that baptism
    and remain worthy of His calling,
Through Jesus Christ our Lord. Amen.
                    (Adapted from Ps. 45:7–9)

The Dismissal

Leader: Go in peace to love and serve the Lord.

Response: Thanks be to God.

SECOND WEEK AFTER EPIPHANY

Call to Worship

Leader: The theme of our worship is that salvation has arrived in God's Son. Hear the word of the Lord: "Behold! The Lamb of God who takes away the sin of the world!" (John 1:29).

Let us pray.

Father, as Your Son, the Lord Jesus Christ, was recognized by John the Baptist, grant that we may in faith acknowledge Him to be Your Son who takes away the sin of the world. Through Christ our Lord, we pray. Amen.

The Scripture Readings

First Reader: A reading from Isaiah:

"And now the LORD says,
Who formed Me from the womb to be His Servant,
To bring Jacob back to Him,
So that Israel is gathered to Him
(For I shall be glorious in the eyes of the LORD,
And My God shall be My strength),

Indeed He says,
'It is too small a thing that You should be My
    Servant
To raise up the tribes of Jacob,
And to restore the preserved ones of Israel;
I will also give You as a light to the Gentiles,
That You should be My salvation to the ends
    of the earth'" (49:5–7).

This is the word of the Lord.

Response: Thanks be to God.

Second   A reading from the gospel of John:
Reader: "The next day John saw Jesus coming toward him, and said, 'Behold! The Lamb of God who takes away the sin of the world! This is He of whom I said, "After me comes a Man who is preferred before me, for He was before me." I did not know Him; but that He should be revealed to Israel, therefore I came baptizing with water.' And John bore witness, saying, 'I saw the Spirit descending from heaven like a dove, and He remained upon Him. I did not know Him, but He who sent me to baptize with water said to me, "Upon whom you see the Spirit descending, and remaining on Him, that is He who baptizes with the Holy Spirit." And I have seen and testified that this is the Son of God'" (1:29–34).

This is the word of the Lord.

Response: Thanks be to God.

The Response

Hymn: *Sing one of the following hymns:*
"Jesus! What a Friend for Sinners!"
"There's within My Heart a Melody"
"Worthy Is the Lamb That Was Slain"

Leader: Let us pray.

Lord, we have waited patiently for You,
And You have heard our cry
   and brought us up out of a horrible pit,
Out of the miry clay.
You have set our feet upon the rock,
Established our steps,
And put a new song in our mouths.
Hear us, O Lord, through Jesus,
The lamb that takes away the sin of the world.
                    (Adapted from Ps. 40:1–3).

The Dismissal

Leader: The grace of God which was given to you by
Jesus Christ will confirm you to the end, that
you may be blameless in the day of our Lord
Jesus Christ (adapted from 1 Cor. 1:4, 8).

Response: Thanks be to God.

THIRD WEEK AFTER EPIPHANY

Leader: The theme of our worship is the beginning of
Jesus' ministry in Galilee. "Follow Me, and I
will make you fishers of men" (Matt. 4:19).

Let us pray.

Father, we celebrate the beginning of Your Son's ministry in Galilee. As He called the disciples to Himself, may we, like them, drop our nets and follow Him, through Christ our Lord. Amen.

The Scripture Readings

First A reading from Isaiah:
Reader: "In Galilee of the Gentiles.
The people who walked in darkness
Have seen a great light;
Those who dwelt in the land of the shadow of
    death,
Upon them a light has shined.
You have multiplied the nation
And increased its joy;
They rejoice before You
According to the joy of harvest,
As men rejoice when they divide the spoil.
For You have broken the yoke of his burden
And the staff of his shoulder,
The rod of his oppressor,
As in the day of Midian" (9:1–4).

This is the word of the Lord.

Response: Thanks be to God.

Second A reading from Matthew:
Reader: "Now when Jesus heard that John had been put in prison, He departed to Galilee. . . .
From that time Jesus began to preach and to

say, 'Repent, for the kingdom of heaven is at hand.' Now Jesus, walking by the Sea of Galilee, saw two brothers, Simon called Peter, and Andrew his brother, casting a net into the sea; for they were fishermen. And He said to them, 'Follow Me, and I will make you fishers of men.' Then they immediately left their nets and followed Him. And going on from there, He saw two other brothers, James the son of Zebedee, and John his brother, in the boat with Zebedee their father, mending their nets. And He called them, and immediately they left the boat and their father, and followed Him. Now Jesus went about all Galilee, teaching in their synagogues, preaching the gospel of the kingdom, and healing all kinds of sickness and all kinds of disease among the people" (4:12, 17–23).

This is the word of the Lord.

Response: Thanks be to God.

The Response

Hymn: *Sing one of the following hymns:*
"Jesus Calls Us O'er the Tumult"
"Go, Tell It on the Mountain"
"Lord, Make Me an Instrument"

Leader: Let us pray.

Lord, do not hide your face from us, or turn away in anger.
Do not leave us nor forsake us,

O God of our salvation.
Lord, You are our light and salvation,
Whom shall we fear?
You are the strength of our lives;
Of whom shall we be afraid?
Lord, we lift up our heads,
    and we sing praises to You.
Hear us, O Lord,
    and have mercy upon us.
For Christ's sake. Amen.

(Adapted from Ps. 27:1–9)

The Dismissal

Leader: Follow after Jesus and "be perfectly joined to-gether in the same mind and in the same judgment" (1 Cor. 1:10).

Response: Thanks be to God.

FOURTH WEEK AFTER EPIPHANY

Call to Worship

Leader: The theme of our worship is that God chooses the poor. Hear the word of the Lord: "Blessed are the poor in spirit,/For theirs is the king-dom of heaven" (Matt. 5:3).

Let us pray.

Father, You look upon the poor and needy and

despise them not. Help us, Lord, to be ever mindful of the needs of others, through Jesus Christ our Lord. Amen.

The Scripture Readings

First
Reader:
A reading from Micah:
"With what shall I come before
     the LORD,
And bow myself before the High God?
Shall I come before Him with burnt offerings,
With calves a year old?
Will the LORD be pleased with thousands of
    rams
Or ten thousand rivers of oil?
Shall I give my firstborn for my transgression,
The fruit of my body for the sin of my soul?
He has shown you, O man, what is good;
And what does the LORD require of you
But to do justly,
To love mercy,
And to walk humbly with your God?"
    (6:6–8).

This is the word of the Lord.

Response: Thanks be to God.

Second
Reader:
A reading from Matthew:
"And seeing the multitudes, He went up on a mountain, and when He was seated His disciples came to Him. Then He opened His mouth and taught them, saying:
'Blessed are the poor in spirit,
    For theirs is the kingdom of heaven,

Blessed are those who mourn,
For they shall be comforted,
Blessed are the meek,
For they shall inherit the earth.
Blessed are those who hunger and thirst for
righteousness,
For they shall be filled.
Blessed are the merciful,
For they shall obtain mercy.
Blessed are the pure in heart,
For they shall see God.
Blessed are the peacemakers,
For they shall be called sons of God.
Blessed are those who are persecuted for
righteousness' sake,
For theirs is the kingdom of heaven.
Blessed are you when they revile and per-
secute you, and say all kinds of evil against
you falsely for My sake. Rejoice and be ex-
ceedingly glad, for great is your reward in
heaven, for so they persecuted the prophets
who were before you'" (Matt. 5:1–12).

This is the word of the Lord.

Response: Thanks be to God.

The Response

Hymn: *Sing one of the following hymns:*
"All People That on Earth Do Dwell"
"I'd Rather Have Jesus"
"My Jesus, I Love Thee"

Leader: Let us pray.

Father, keep us from listening to the counsel
of the ungodly,
From walking in the path of sinners,
Or sitting in the seat of the scornful.
Teach us to delight in Your law
And to meditate upon it day and night.
Make us like a tree planted by nourishing
water,
Yielding luscious fruit,
Blessed with strong, shiny leaves
And prospering in all that we do.
Let us not be like the ungodly
Who are like the chaff which the wind drives
away,
Who will not be able to stand strong on the
day of judgment
Nor sit in the congregation of the righteous;
For You know the way of the righteous,
And the way of the ungodly shall perish.
Amen.

(Adapted from Ps. 1)

The Dismissal

Leader: "God has chosen the foolish things of the
world to put to shame the wise, and God
has chosen the weak things of the world to
put to shame the things which are mighty"
(1 Cor. 1:27).

Response: Thanks be to God.

FIFTH WEEK AFTER EPIPHANY

Call to Worship

Leader: The theme of our worship today is God's call for us to be the salt of the earth and the light of the world. Hear the word of the Lord: "You are the salt of the earth. . . . You are the light of the world" (Matt. 5:13–14).

Let us pray.

Lord, as Your Son, the Lord Jesus Christ, was salt and light here on earth, so help us who walk in His way to so serve and minister to the needs of others that we may be salt with flavor and a light set upon a hill. We ask this through Jesus our Lord. Amen.

The Scripture Readings

First
Reader:

A reading from Isaiah:

"Is this not the fast that I have chosen:
To loose the bonds of wickedness,
To undo the heavy burdens,
To let the oppressed go free,
And that you break every yoke?
Is it not to share your bread with the hungry,
And that you bring to your house the poor
    who are cast out;
When you see the naked, that you cover him,
And not hide yourself from your own flesh?
Then your light shall break forth like the
    morning,

Your healing shall spring forth speedily,
And your righteousness shall go before you;
The glory of the LORD shall be your rear
    guard.
Then you shall call, and the LORD will
    answer;
You shall cry, and He will say, 'Here I am'"
    (58:6–9).

This is the word of the Lord.

Response: Thanks be to God.

Second   A reading from Matthew:
Reader: "You are the salt of the earth; but if the salt loses its flavor, how shall it be seasoned? It is then good for nothing but to be thrown out and trampled underfoot by men. You are the light of the world. A city that is set on a hill cannot be hidden. Nor do they light a lamp and put it under a basket, but on a lampstand, and it gives light to all who are in the house. Let your light so shine before men, that they may see your good works and glorify your Father in heaven" (5:13–16).

This is the word of the Lord.

Response: Thanks be to God.

The Response

Hymn: *Sing one of the following hymns:*
        "Take My Life and Let It Be"
        "The Light of the World Is Jesus"
        "I'll Live for Him Who Died for Me"

Leader: Let us pray.

Father, bless those who fear You and keep Your commandments.

Bless those who are full of compassion and righteousness.

Bless those who guide their affairs with discretion,

Who give to the poor,

Whose heart is steadfast in You.

We pray through Jesus Christ our Lord. Amen.

(Adapted from Ps. 112)

The Dismissal

Leader: "Let your light so shine before men, that they may see your good works and glorify your Father in heaven" (Matt. 5:16).

Response: Thanks be to God.

SIXTH WEEK AFTER EPIPHANY

Call to Worship

Leader: The theme of our worship today is the freedom we have to choose the love of God as our way of life. Hear the word of the Lord: "Love the LORD your God . . . obey His voice and . . . cling to Him" (Deut. 30:20).

Let us pray.

Lord God, You who are eternal love, You who out of Your love became one of us, You who by Your incarnate example show love, grant us, we pray, the freedom to love You with our whole heart, mind, and body, by being obedient to Your will in all things. Through Jesus Christ our Lord we pray. Amen.

The Scripture Readings

First   A reading from Deuteronomy:
Reader: "See, I have set before you today life and good, death and evil, in that I command you today to love the LORD your God, to walk in His ways, and to keep His commandments, His statutes, and His judgments, that you may live and multiply; and the LORD your God will bless you in the land which you go to possess. But if your heart turns away so that you do not hear, and are drawn away, and worship other gods and serve them, I announce to you today that you shall surely perish; you shall not prolong your days in the land which you cross over the Jordan to go in and possess. I call heaven and earth as witnesses today against you, that I have set before you life and death, blessing and cursing; therefore choose life, that both you and your descendants may live; that you may love the LORD your God, that you may obey His voice, and that you may cling to Him, for He is your life and the length of your days; and that you may dwell in the land which the LORD swore to your fa-

thers, to Abraham, Isaac, and Jacob, to give them" (30:15–20).

This is the word of the Lord.

Response: Thanks be to God.

Second Reader: A reading from Matthew:

"You have heard that it was said to those of old, 'You shall not murder,' and whoever murders will be in danger of the judgment. But I say to you that whoever is angry with his brother without a cause shall be in danger of the judgment. . . . You have heard that it was said to those of old, 'You shall not commit adultery.' But I say to you that whoever looks at a woman to lust for her has already committed adultery with her in his heart. And if your right eye causes you to sin, pluck it out and cast it from you; for it is more profitable for you that one of your members perish, than for your whole body to be cast into hell. And if your right hand causes you to sin, cut it off and cast it from you; for it is more profitable for you that one of your members perish, than for your whole body to be cast into hell. . . . Let your 'Yes' be 'Yes,' and your 'No,' 'No.' For whatever is more than these is from the evil one" (5:21–22, 27–30, 37).

This is the word of the Lord.

Response: Thanks be to God.

The Response

Hymn: *Sing one of the following hymns:*
"My Jesus, I Love Thee"
"I Would Be Like Jesus"
"There's Something about That Name"

Let us pray.

Holy Father, You who are perfect in all Your ways,
Lead us into the cleansing of our ways.
May we take heed to Your word;
May we seek You with our whole heart.
O Lord, keep us from wandering from Your commands,
May Your word be hidden in our hearts,
That we might not sin against You.
Lord, we will meditate on Your precepts.
We will contemplate Your ways.
We will delight in Your statutes;
We will not forget Your word.
Through Jesus, our redeemer and example, we pray. Amen.

(Adaptation of Ps. 119:9–16)

The Dismissal

Leader: Blessed are those who walk in the law of the Lord. And blessed are they who seek Him with the whole heart!

(Adaptation of Ps. 119:1–2)

Response: Thanks be to God.

SEVENTH WEEK AFTER EPIPHANY

Call to Worship

Leader: The theme of our worship today is the love of neighbor and the love of our enemies. Hear the word of the Lord: "I say to you, love your enemies, bless those who curse you, do good to those who hate you, and pray for those who spitefully use you and persecute you" (Matt. 5:44).

Let us pray.

Almighty God, we, Your unworthy servants, acknowledge Your everlasting love. Even though we had fallen into sin and did not love You, You loved us and gave Your Son to redeem us. Teach us, O heavenly One, to love with Christ-love. May our love extend to family, friends, neighbors, yes, even to our enemies, through Jesus Christ who loved us and gave Himself for us. Amen.

The Scripture Readings

First Reader: A reading from Leviticus:

"And the LORD spoke to Moses, saying, 'Speak to all the congregation of the children of Israel, and say to them: "You shall be holy, for I the LORD your God am holy. . . . You shall not hate your brother in your heart. You shall surely rebuke your neighbor, and not bear sin because of him. You shall not take vengeance, nor bear any grudge against the children of your people, but you shall love your neighbor as yourself: I am the LORD"'" (19:1–2, 17–18).

This is the word of the Lord.

Response: Thanks be to God.

Second Reader: A reading from Matthew:

"You have heard that it was said, 'An eye for an eye and a tooth for a tooth.' But I tell you not to resist an evil person. But whoever slaps you on your right cheek, turn the other to him also. If anyone wants to sue you and take away your tunic, let him have your cloak also. And whoever compels you to go one mile, go with him two. Give to him who asks you, and from him who wants to borrow from you do not turn away. You have heard that it was said, 'You shall love your neighbor and hate your enemy.' But I say to you, love your enemies, bless those who curse you, do good to those who hate you, and pray for those who spitefully use you and persecute you, that you may be sons of your Father in heaven; for He makes His sun rise on the evil and on the good, and sends rain on the just and on the unjust. For if you love those who love you, what reward have you? Do not even the tax collectors do the same? And if you greet your brethren only, what do you do more than others? Do not even the tax collectors do so?

Therefore you shall be perfect, just as your Father in heaven is perfect" (5:38–48).

This is the word of the Lord.

Response: Thanks be to God.

The Response

Hymn: *Sing one of the following hymns:*
"More Like Jesus Would I Be"
"Living for Jesus"
"Seek Ye First"

Leader: Let us pray.

Bless the Lord, O my soul;
And all that is within me, bless His holy
      name!
Bless the Lord, O my soul,
And forget not all His benefits,
Who forgives all our iniquities,
Who heals all our diseases,
Who redeems our life from destruction,
Who crowns us with lovingkindness and
      tender mercies,
Who satisfies our mouth with good things,
So that our youth is renewed like the eagle's.
For as the heavens are high above the earth,
So great is His mercy toward those who fear
      Him.
As far as the east is from the west,
So far has He removed our transgressions from
      us.
As a father pities his children,

So the Lord pities those who fear Him.
Amen.

(Adaptation of Ps. 103:1–5, 11–13)

The Dismissal

Leader: Go in peace to love and serve the Lord.

Response: Thanks be to God.

EIGHTH WEEK AFTER EPIPHANY

Call to Worship

Leader: The theme of our worship today is the loving
providence of God. Hear the word of the
Lord: "Do not worry about tomorrow, for tomorrow will worry about its own things"
(Matt. 6:34).

Let us pray.

Lord, we Your creatures are prone to the cares
of this world. Teach us, through the birds of
the air who lack for nothing and the lilies of
the field that grow without toil, to trust in
You, through Jesus Christ our Lord. Amen.

The Scripture Readings

First
Reader: A reading from Isaiah:
"Sing, O heavens!
Be joyful, O earth!

And break out in singing, O mountains!
For the LORD has comforted His people,
And will have mercy on His afflicted.
But Zion said,
'The LORD has forsaken me,
And my Lord has forgotten me.'
'Can a woman forget her nursing child,
And not have compassion on the son of her
    womb?
Surely they may forget,
Yet I will not forget you.
See, I have inscribed you on the palms of My
    hands;
Your walls are continually before Me.
Your sons shall make haste;
Your destroyers and those who laid you waste
Shall go away from you.
Lift up your eyes, look around and see;
All these gather together and come to you.
As I live,' says the LORD,
'You shall surely clothe yourselves with them
    all as an ornament,
And bind them on you as a bride does'"
    (49:13–18).

This is the word of the Lord.

Response: Thanks be to God.

Second   A reading from Matthew:
Reader: "No one can serve two masters; for either he
will hate the one and love the other, or else he
will be loyal to the one and despise the other.
You cannot serve God and mammon. There-

fore I say to you, do not worry about your life, what you will eat or what you will drink; nor about your body, what you will put on. Is not life more than food and the body more than clothing? Look at the birds of the air, for they neither sow nor reap nor gather into barns; yet your heavenly Father feeds them. Are you not of more value than they? Which of you by worrying can add one cubit to his stature? So why do you worry about clothing? Consider the lilies of the field, how they grow: they neither toil nor spin; and yet I say to you that even Solomon in all his glory was not arrayed like one of these. Now if God so clothes the grass of the field, which today is, and tomorrow is thrown into the oven, will He not much more clothe you, O you of little faith? Therefore do not worry, saying, 'What shall we eat?' or 'What shall we drink?' or 'What shall we wear?' For after all these things the Gentiles seek. For your heavenly Father knows that you need all these things. But seek first the kingdom of God and His righteousness, and all these things shall be added to you" (6:24–33).

The Response

Hymn: *Sing one of the following hymns:*
"Be Still, My Soul"
"Near the Cross"
"Peace, Peace, Wonderful Peace"

Leader: Let us pray.

Lord, our souls wait silently for You;
For You are our rock and our salvation,
The rock of our strength.
Let us not trust in the plans of men
Nor in the increase of riches, O Lord.
But let us trust in You at all times,
For power belongs to You and You alone.
Amen.

(Adaptation of Ps. 62)

The Dismissal

Leader: Trust in the Lord with all your heart and lean on Him alone.

Response: Thanks be to God.

LAST WEEK OF EPIPHANY

Call to Worship

Leader: The theme of this week is the glory of Christ with the Father. Hear the words of the Lord: "His face shone like the sun, and His clothes became as white as the light" (Matt. 17:2).

Let us pray.

Lord Jesus, You are one with the Father, yet You set aside Your glory to become one of us. Let us, O bright Light of Glory, share in the vision of Your glory. Let us see You and worship You in the glory You have with the Father. Amen.

The Scripture Reading

First Reader: A reading from Exodus:

"Then the LORD said to Moses, 'Come up to Me on the mountain and be there; and I will give you tablets of stone, and the law and commandments which I have written, that you may teach them.' So Moses arose with his assistant Joshua, and Moses went up to the mountain of God. And he said to the elders, 'Wait here for us until we come back to you. Indeed Aaron and Hur are with you. If any man has a difficulty, let him go to them.' Then Moses went up into the mountain, and a cloud covered the mountain. Now the glory of the LORD rested on Mount Sinai, and the cloud covered it six days. And on the seventh day He called to Moses out of the midst of the cloud. The sight of the glory of the LORD was like a consuming fire on the top of the mountain in the eyes of the children of Israel. So Moses went into the midst of the cloud and went up into the mountain. And Moses was on the mountain forty days and forty nights" (24:12–18).

This is the word of the Lord.

Response: Thanks be to God.

Second Reader: A reading from Matthew:

"Now after six days Jesus took Peter, James,

and John his brother, brought them up on a high mountain by themselves, and was transfigured before them. His face shone like the sun, and His clothes became as white as the light. And behold, Moses and Elijah appeared to them, talking with Him. Then Peter answered and said to Jesus, 'Lord, it is good for us to be here; if You wish, let us make here three tabernacles: one for You, one for Moses, and one for Elijah.' While he was still speaking, behold, a bright cloud overshadowed them; and suddenly a voice came out of the cloud, saying, 'This is My beloved Son, in whom I am well pleased. Hear Him!' And when the disciples heard it, they fell on their faces and were greatly afraid. But Jesus came and touched them and said, 'Arise, and do not be afraid.' And when they had lifted up their eyes, they saw no one but Jesus only. Now as they came down from the mountain, Jesus commanded them, saying, 'Tell the vision to no one until the Son of Man is risen from the dead'" (17:1–9).

This is the word of the Lord.

Response: Thanks be to God.

The Response

Hymn: *Sing one of the following hymns:*
"O Radiant Light, O Sun Divine"
"Crown Him with Many Crowns"
"Our God Reigns"

Leader: Let us pray.

Father, we have heard the decree:
"You are My Son."
Lord, grant Your Son His inheritance,
The ends of the earth for His possession,
Let Him rule with the rod of iron
and bend us all to kiss the Son
Lest He be angry
And we perish in the way. Amen.

(Adapted from Ps. 2:7–13)

The Dismissal

Leader: "Blessed are all those who put their trust in Him" (Ps. 2:12).

Response: Thanks be to God.

LENT

LENT This figure was designed to communicate the season of penitence. The upswept "arms" have been associated with a sense of hope and longing. Note the modified triangle—a theme which is easily recognized as the Godhead minus one angle.

INTRODUCTION TO
Eastertide and Lent

Eastertide

Eastertide, the second festive season of the year, includes Lent, Holy Week, Easter, and ends with Pentecost. The overriding theme of Eastertide is expressed in another name used for this season, the *Cycle of Life*. The Cycle of Life takes us into the death of Christ and brings us out on the other side with the resurrection.

The central event of the season is Easter Sunday, known in the early church as *Pascha* or the "Christian Passover." Paul wrote, "For indeed Christ, our Passover, was sacrificed for us" (1 Cor. 5:7). Easter is the most festive commemoration of the Christian church because, like Passover, it commemorates a deliverance from the powers of evil and a redemption to a new life. For this reason the early church made Easter the day *par excellence* for baptism. The symbol of baptism expressed by Paul in Romans 6 is as a death and burial with Jesus Christ and a rising in His resurrection; therefore it is a most appropriate sacrament for this day.

Because the practice of baptism into Christ's death dominated the church's spiritual pilgrimage toward

Easter, baptism themes such as fasting, repentance, prayer, intensive involvement in the mystery of Christ, and personal spiritual renewal became the major elements of the church's journey through Lent. The last week, Holy Week, intensified even more the disciplines that assisted the mystery of entrance into Christ's death.

After the resurrection, the spirituality of Easter shifts into a different mood. The focus is no longer sober entrance into the death of Christ, but a joyful celebration of the risen Lord. Therefore, the themes of spiritual discipline after Easter focus on a relationship with the resurrected Christ and culminates in His ascension, the coming of the Holy Spirit, and the birthday of the church. All these themes are reflected in our family worship services of this season.

Lent

Unlike the word *Advent*, which has a religious meaning, *Lent* is a secular word that simply means "spring." However, it has attained religious meaning through its long usage in the church as the time to prepare for Easter.

Lent is the repentance season of the church year. It is a time for spiritual self-examination, turning from sin, and renewal of spiritual life. Originally Lent developed around the catechumens, who were being prepared for their solemn baptism at the great Easter vigil service. Gradually all Christians joined with them as a time to renew their own baptismal covenant with the Lord.

Today during Lent Christians seek to identify with the suffering of Christ. For this reason Christians take on a special discipline during Lent which assists their spiritual pilgrimage into His death and resurrection. Traditionally these special disciplines include prayer, fasting, and alms-giving, the threefold theme of Matthew 6.

Lent begins in the West with Ash Wednesday when Christians are reminded, "Dust you are/And to dust you shall return" (Gen. 3:19). The focus of the first week of readings is on the power of Christ over Satan, a power which will result in His and our victory over the grave.

During the second week the image of Christ as the "Lamb of God who takes away the sin of the world" (John 1:29) is predominant. The antiphon selected for the second week is, "It is Christ who died, and further-more is also risen, who is even at the right hand of God, who also makes intercession for us" (Rom. 8:34). Here Christ's death is connected with His resurrection as it is throughout Lent.

In the third week the family meditation carries us into the freedom from death that comes as a result of Christ's death. This is signified by the sign of the temple, which, if destroyed, Christ will raise in three days. Next, the fourth week emphasizes the new birth, which results from Christ's death and resurrection when we in faith trust in Him as Lord and Savior.

And finally in the last week before Holy Week we are brought face to face with the impending death of Christ. Yet, even here the resurrection as the sign of hope is central in Jesus' teaching: "Unless a grain of wheat falls into the ground and dies, it remains alone; but if it dies, it produces much grain" (John 12:24).

In summary, three items weave their way in and out of these family services during Lent. The impending death of our Lord, the hope of the resurrection, and the neces-sity of faith and trust in Christ. Lent should be seen as a collective retreat for the whole family and for the church at large. It is forty days to relive our entrance into Christ, to repent of our sins, to seek a change of heart and life, and to experience genuine spiritual renewal.

It is important during Lent to encourage each member of the family (even the younger children) to adopt a discipline of prayer, fasting, and almsgiving. Prayer, and attendance and involvement in weekly family services is a good start. If the children are older, encourage a daily discipline of reading and prayer. Lenten books for children are available in most bookstores. A book designed for Lent will obviously organize and order the prayer life better than a haphazard choice of readings.

In regard to food, a family discipline of eating Lenten foods may assist the spiritual pilgrimage. Examples of such foods are hot cross buns, soups such as lentil and spinach soup, and the withdrawal of serving desserts. In this way the discipline around foods works as external help to the inner journey.

Finally, you may want to adopt a tradition of giving charitable gifts to the needy. Place an alms box on the table so that each evening parents and children can donate pocket change that will go to a needy cause. These and other customs you may adopt will not only remind us of our Lenten pilgrimage, but embody the pilgrimage and provide a tangible way to go through Lent. (For the dates of Ash Wednesday and Easter, check Appendix I.)

ASH WEDNESDAY

We Prepare to Worship

Leader: Dear family, we now enter into the most solemn season of the Christian year, Lent. During Lent we identify with the sufferings of Jesus and enter into His death. He calls us to take up His cross and follow Him. We begin on this day, Ash Wednesday, by calling to mind the frailty of our creaturehood.

Let us pray.

Heavenly Father, Creator of all that is, seen and unseen, You know our hearts and innermost thoughts. You know us to be sinners, breakers of the law, and disobedient to Your will. Yet, You in Your Son Jesus Christ became one of us to free us from sin, to bring us back to You. May we, Your humble servants, willingly follow You in Your suffering, so that we, who enter into the tomb with You, may also rise to a glorious resurrection through Jesus Christ our Lord who lives and reigns with You and the Holy Spirit, one God, forever. Amen.

Hymn: *Sing one of the following hymns:*
"Lord, Who throughout These Forty Days"
"Lead Me to Calvary"
"Unto Thee, O Lord, Do I Lift Up My Soul"

We Listen to the Word of God

First   A reading from Joel:
Reader: "'Now, therefore,' says the LORD,
'Turn to me with all your heart,
With fasting, with weeping, and with
       mourning.'
So rend your heart, and not your garments;
Return to the LORD your God,
For He is gracious and merciful,
Slow to anger, and of great kindness;
And He relents from doing harm.
Who knows if He will turn and relent,
And leave a blessing behind Him—
A grain offering and a drink offering
For the LORD your God?
Blow the trumpet in Zion,
Consecrate a fast,
Call a sacred assembly;
Gather the people,
Sanctify the congregation,
Assemble the elders,
Gather the children and nursing babes;
Let the bridegroom go out from his chamber,
And the bride from her dressing room.
Let the priests, who minister to the LORD,
Weep between the porch and the altar;
Let them say, 'Spare Your people, O Lord,

And do not give Your heritage to reproach,
That the nations should rule over them.
Why should they say among the peoples,
"Where is their God?"'
Then the LORD will be zealous for His land,
And pity His people.
The LORD will answer and say to His people,
'Behold, I will send you grain and new wine
      and oil,
And you will be satisfied by them;
I will no longer make you a reproach among
      the nations'" (2:12–19).

This is the word of the Lord.

Response: Thanks be to God.

Second　A reading from the gospel of Matthew:
Reader:　"Take heed that you do not do your charitable
deeds before men, to be seen by them. Other-
wise you have no reward from your Father in
heaven. Therefore, when you do a charitable
deed, do not sound a trumpet before you as
the hypocrites do in the synagogues and in the
streets, that they may have glory from men.
Assuredly, I say to you, they have their reward. But when you do a charitable deed, do
not let your left hand know what your right
hand is doing, that your charitable deed may
be in secret; and your Father who sees in secret will Himself reward you openly" (6:1–4).

This is the word of the Lord.

Response: Thanks be to God.

We Respond to the Word of God

The Inquiry and Instruction

Question: What is the meaning of the word *Lent?*

Answer: It has no religious meaning like *Advent* or *Pentecost.* It comes from an Anglo-Saxon word, *lencten,* meaning "spring."

Question: Why do we observe Lent?

Answer: The purpose of Lent is to provide a time for us to enter into the suffering of Jesus and to go with Him into the tomb.

Question: How can we do this?

Answer: The experience of the people of God who have gone before us is that we best identify with Jesus by adopting a discipline of prayer, fasting, and almsgiving.

Question: How should we pray?

Answer: Our prayer may be a spiritual meditation on Jesus Christ—His teaching, His suffering, His death on our behalf.

Question: Why should we fast?

Answer: Fasting is an aid to prayer. Years ago Augustine wrote, "When a man imposes on himself the burden of fasting, he shows that he really wants what he is asking for." Christians fast in order to pray more intently.

Question: What is the purpose of almsgiving?

Answer: We give alms to the poor and needy because it is a specific expression of the brotherly love produced by prayer. The closer we are to Jesus, the more we care for our neighbor.

The Prayer of Response

Leader: Let us pray.

"Have mercy upon me, O God,
According to Your lovingkindness;
According to the multitude of Your tender
   mercies,
Blot out my transgressions.
Wash me thoroughly from my iniquity,
And cleanse me from my sin. . . .
Create in me a clean heart, O God,
And renew a steadfast spirit within me.
Do not cast me away from Your presence,
And do not take Your Holy Spirit from me.
Restore to me the joy of Your salvation,
And uphold me with Your generous Spirit"
(Ps. 51:1–2, 10–12).

All: Amen.

We Are Sent Forth

Leader: I "plead with you not to receive the grace of God in vain. For He says: 'In an acceptable time I have heard you,/And in the day of salvation I have helped you'" (2 Cor. 6:1–2).

Response: Thanks be to God.

FIRST WEEK IN LENT

We Prepare to Worship God

Leader: In this the first week of Lent we focus on the temptation of Christ. He who came to overcome the devil, to destroy his kingdom, and, to establish the kingdom of God forever, confronted the devil and resisted his temptation. This He did for us, to break Satan's power in our lives and set us free to serve Him.

Let us pray.

Father, You sent Your Son to destroy the devil, to tread down hell, and to loose us from our sin. Grant that we, who are daily tempted, may draw on the power of Christ. May we, like Him, resist the evil one, turn from temptation, and find solace in Your word. Through Jesus Christ our Lord we pray. Amen.

Hymn: *Sing one of the following hymns:*
"As You with Satan Did Content"
"Yield Not to Temptation"
"He Is Lord"

We Listen to the Word of God

First
Reader: A reading from Genesis:
"Now the serpent was more cunning than any beast of the field which the LORD God had made. And he said to the woman, 'Has God

indeed said, "You shall not eat of every tree of the garden?"' And the woman said to the serpent, 'We may eat the fruit of the trees of the garden; but the fruit of the tree which is in the midst of the garden, God has said, "You shall not eat it, nor shall you touch it, lest you die."' And the serpent said to the woman, 'You will not surely die. For God knows that in the day you eat of it your eyes will be opened, and you will be like God, knowing good and evil.' So when the woman saw that the tree was good for food, that it was pleasant to the eyes, and a tree desirable to make one wise, she took of its fruit and ate. She also gave to her husband with her, and he ate. Then the eyes of both of them were opened, and they knew that they were naked; and they sewed fig leaves together and made themselves coverings. And they heard the sound of the LORD God walking in the garden in the cool of the day, and Adam and his wife hid themselves from the presence of the LORD God among the trees of the garden." (3:1–8).

This is the word of the Lord.

Response: Thanks be to God.

Second Reader: A reading from the gospel of Matthew:
"Then Jesus was led up by the Spirit into the wilderness to be tempted by the devil. And when He had fasted forty days and forty nights, afterward He was hungry. Now when the tempter came to Him, he said, 'If You are

the Son of God, command that these stones become bread.' But He answered and said, 'It is written, "Man shall not live by bread alone, but by every word that proceeds from the mouth of God."' Then the devil took Him up into the holy city, set Him on the pinnacle of the temple, and said to Him, 'If You are the Son of God, throw Yourself down. For it is written: "He shall give his angels charge concerning you," and, "In their hands they shall bear you up/Lest you dash your foot against a stone."' Jesus said to him, 'It is written again, "You shall not tempt the LORD your God."' Again, the devil took Him up on an exceedingly high mountain, and showed Him all the kingdoms of the world and their glory. And he said to Him, 'All these things I will give You if You will fall down and worship me.' Then Jesus said to him, 'Away with you, Satan! For it is written, "You shall worship the LORD your God, and Him only you shall serve."' Then the devil left Him, and behold, angels came and ministered to Him" (4:1–11).

This is the word of the Lord.

Response: Thanks be to God.

We Respond to the Word of God

The Inquiry and Instruction

Question: Why do we focus on the temptation of Christ during Lent?

Answer: The temptation is closely linked to the death of Christ.

Question: How?

Answer: Christ came to destroy the kingdom of the devil by His death. In the beginning of His ministry He showed His power over evil and the evil one.

Question: Why is this important to us during Lent?

Answer: For two reasons. First, you cannot understand the ministry of Jesus, which we celebrate during Lent, unless you know that Jesus has already given Satan notice of his sure doom. Jesus' ministry of casting out demons and healing the sick is possible only because he has already gained power over the evil one.

Question: What is the second reason?

Answer: The second reason why we celebrate Christ's power over evil during Lent has to do with us. He gives us His victory so that we too can overcome the temptation of sin that comes our way.

The Prayers of Response

Leader: Let us pray.

Lord, do not remember the sins of our youth,
Nor our transgressions.
According to Your mercy remember us,
For Your goodness' sake, O Lord.
Show us Your ways, O Lord;

Teach us Your paths.
Lead us in Your truth and teach us,
For You are the God of our salvation;
On You we wait all the day.
To You, O Lord, we lift up our soul.
O our God, we trust in You. Amen.

(Adaptation of Ps. 25:4–7)

We Are Sent Forth

Leader: Go and sin no more.

Response: Thanks be to God.

SECOND WEEK IN LENT

We Prepare to Worship

Leader: During this solemn second week of Lent we see Jesus as the sacrifice, the spotless victim, whom the Father offers on our behalf. He alone, the God-man, is able to reconcile man to God and God to man for, "it is Christ who died, and furthermore is also risen, who is even at the right hand of God, who also makes intercession for us" (Rom. 8:34).

Let us pray.

Father, You gave Your only begotten Son, the Lord Jesus Christ, to live and die for us, that we who believe in Him may also follow Him in life and death. May we die to our sinful self, and may we rise to new life in Him who conquered sin, that we might have life more abundantly. Through Jesus, we pray. Amen.

Hymn: *Sing one of the following hymns:*
"As You Did Hunger and Did Thirst"
"Alas, and Did My Savior Bleed"
"And Can It Be"

We Listen to the Word of God

First Reader: A reading from Genesis:
"Now it came to pass after these things that God tested Abraham, and said to him, 'Abraham!' And he said, 'Here I am.' And He said, 'Take now your son, your only son Isaac, whom you love, and go to the land of Moriah, and offer him there as a burnt offering on one of the mountains of which I shall tell you.' Then they came to the place of which God had told him. And Abraham built an altar there and placed the wood in order; and he bound Isaac his son and laid him on the altar, upon the wood. And Abraham stretched out his hand and took the knife to slay his son. But the Angel of the LORD called him from heaven and said, 'Abraham, Abraham!' And he said, 'Here I am,' And He said, 'Do not lay your hand on the lad, or do anything to him; for now I know that you fear God, seeing you have not withheld your son, your only son, from Me.' Then Abraham lifted his eyes and looked, and there was behind him a ram

caught in a thicket by its horns. So Abraham went and took the ram, and offered it up for a burnt offering instead of his son. And Abraham called the name of the place, The-LORD-Will-Provide; as it is said to this day, 'In the Mount of the LORD it shall be provided.' Then the Angel of the LORD called to Abraham a second time out of heaven, and said: 'By Myself I have sworn, says the LORD, because you have done this thing, and have not withheld your son, your only son, in blessing I will bless you, and in multiplying your descendants as the stars of the heaven and as the sand which is on the seashore; and your descendants shall possess the gate of their enemies. In your seed all the nations of the earth shall be blessed, because you have obeyed My voice'" (22:1–2, 9–18).

This is the word of the Lord.

Response: Thanks be to God.

Second Reader: A reading from the gospel of Mark:

"And He began to teach them that the Son of Man must suffer many things, and be rejected by the elders and chief priests and scribes, and be killed, and after three days rise again. He spoke this word openly. And Peter took Him aside and began to rebuke Him. But when He had turned around and looked at His disciples, He rebuked Peter, saying, 'Get behind Me, Satan! For you are not mindful of the things of God, but the things of men.' And when He had called the people to Him, with His disciples also, He said to them, 'Whoever desires to come after Me, let him deny himself, and take up his cross, and follow Me. For whoever desires to save his life will lose it, but whoever loses his life for My sake and the gospel's will save it. For what will it profit a man if he gains the whole world, and loses his own soul? Or what will a man give in exchange for his soul? For whoever is ashamed of Me and My words in this adulterous and sinful generation, of him the Son of Man also will be ashamed when He comes in the glory of His Father with the holy angels'" (8:31–38).

This is the word of the Lord.

Response: Thanks be to God.

We Respond to the Word of God

The Inquiry and Instruction

Question: I don't understand why God would ask Abraham to sacrifice his son.

Answer: It was both a test and a type.

Question: Who was God testing?

Answer: Abraham's faith and trust in God was being tested. For years Abraham had prayed for a son. God answered that prayer. Now God wanted to see whether Abraham was willing to give up his most treasured possession for Him.

Question: Does this example have any meaning for us?

Answer: Yes, through it God asks us what we are willing to sacrifice for Him. That's a good question to ponder during Lent.

Question: Did you say the story is also a type?

Answer: Yes, Isaac is a type of Christ. God gave His only Son up for sacrifice to free us from our sin.

The Prayer of Response

Leader: Let us pray.

> Lord, we love You because You have heard
> Our voice and our supplications,
> Because You have inclined Your ear to us.
> Therefore we will call upon You as long as we
> live.
> We will offer to You the sacrifice of
> thanksgiving,
> And will call upon the name of the Lord.
> We will pay our vows to the Lord
> Now in the presence of all Your people,
> In the courts of Your house. Amen.
> (Adaptation of Ps. 116:1–2, 13–19)

We Are Sent Forth

Leader: "If God is for us, who can be against us?" (Rom. 8:31).

Response: Thanks be to God.

THIRD WEEK IN LENT

We Prepare to Worship

Leader: During this week God calls us to meditate on the liberation He brings us through Jesus Christ. Though our Lord was to be put to death, He alone knew that death could not hold Him in the grave. He would rise again on the third day, and we who are in Him by faith have been raised to newness of life.

Let us pray.

Father, during this long night of Lent we, Your servants, are becoming increasingly conscious of our sin. Lord, we do not ask to be relieved of this burden, for our sin nailed You to the cross, yet You set us free by Your Son's death and resurrection. For this and all Your benefits, we bless Your holy name, through Christ our Lord. Amen.

Hymn: *Sing one of the following hymns:*
"The Glory of These Forty Days"
"The Old Rugged Cross"
"I Know the Lord Will Make a Way for Me"

We Listen to the Word of God

First Reader: A reading from Exodus:
"And God spoke all these words, saying:
'I am the LORD your God, who brought you

out of the land of Egypt, out of the house of bondage.

'You shall have no other gods before Me.

'You shall not make for yourself any carved image, or any likeness of anything that is in the heaven above, or that is in the earth beneath, or that is in the water under the earth; you shall not bow down to them nor serve them. For I, the LORD your God, am a jealous God, visiting the iniquity of the fathers on the children to the third and fourth generations of those who hate Me, but showing mercy to thousands, to those who love Me and keep My commandments.

'You shall not take the name of the LORD your God in vain, for the LORD will not hold him guiltless who takes His name in vain.

'Remember the Sabbath day, to keep it holy. Six days you shall labor and do all your work, but the seventh day is the Sabbath of the LORD your God. In it you shall do no work: you, nor your son, nor your daughter, nor your manservant, nor your maidservant, nor your cattle, nor your stranger who is within your gates. For in six days the LORD made the heavens and the earth, the sea, and all that is in them, and rested the seventh day. Therefore the LORD blessed the Sabbath day and hallowed it.

'Honor your father and your mother, that your

days may be long upon the land which the LORD your God is giving you.

'You shall not murder.

'You shall not commit adultery.

'You shall not steal.

'You shall not bear false witness against your neighbor.

'You shall not covet your neighbor's house; you shall not covet your neighbor's wife, nor his manservant, nor his maidservant, nor his ox, nor his donkey, nor anything that is your neighbor's'" (20:1–17).

This is the word of the Lord.

Response: Thanks be to God.

Second Reader: A reading from the gospel of John:

"Now the Passover of the Jews was at hand, and Jesus went up to Jerusalem. And He found in the temple those who sold oxen and sheep and doves, and the moneychangers doing business. When He had made a whip of cords, He drove them all out of the temple, with the sheep and oxen, and poured out the changers' money and overturned the tables. And He said to those who sold doves, 'Take these things away! Do not make My Father's house a house of merchandise!' Then His disciples remembered that it was written, 'Zeal for Your house has eaten Me up.' So the Jews answered and said to Him, 'What sign do You show to us, since You do these things?' Jesus answered and said to them, 'Destroy this temple, and in three days I will raise it up.' Then the Jews said, 'It has taken forty-six years to build this temple, and will You raise it up in three days?' But He was speaking of the temple of His body. Therefore, when He had risen from the dead, His disciples remembered that He had said this to them; and they believed the Scripture and the word which Jesus had said" (2:13–22).

This is the word of the Lord.

Response: Thanks be to God.

We Respond to the Word of God

The Inquiry and Instruction

Question: Why did we read the Ten Commandments?

Answer: God gave us the commandments to increase our sense of sin.

Question: What do you mean?

Answer: No one, no matter how good or moral they are, is able to keep the Ten Commandments.

Question: Then why did God give them to us?

Answer: The Ten Commandments lead us to Christ. Paul refers to the commandments as "our tutor to bring us to Christ, that we might be justified by faith" (Gal. 3:24).

Question: You mean my Lenten discipline won't bring me to salvation?

Answer: Exactly. Only Christ, who was put to death and rose again, even as He predicted in our gospel reading for today, can save us.

Question: Then why should I keep a Lenten discipline?

Answer: Awareness of your sin and forgiveness will increase your reliance on Christ for your salvation.

The Prayer of Response

Leader: Let us pray.

Lord, cleanse us from secret faults.
Keep us from presumptuous sins;
Let them not have dominion over us.
Then we shall be blameless,
And we shall be innocent of great
    transgression.
Let the words of our mouths and the
    meditations of our hearts
Be acceptable in Your sight,
O Lord, our strength and our redeemer.
(Adaptation of Ps. 19:12–14)

We Are Sent Forth

Leader: In Christ you have been set free.

Response: Thanks be to God.

FOURTH WEEK IN LENT

We Prepare to Worship God

Leader: During this most solemn week our minds and hearts are turned toward the new life in Christ. He came not to condemn us but to renew and restore us. He comes not only as the judge against sin and all unrighteousness, but also, as the Great Physician, He calls us to Himself, to repentance and conversion.

Let us pray.

Lord God, through Your Son a word of peace was brought to the world. May we who confess His name bring that reconciliation to the world. Through the spiritual discipline we have taken, make us instruments of Your peace, through Jesus Christ our Lord. Amen.

Hymn: *Sing one of the following hymns:*
"With Broken Heart and Contrite Sigh"
"O Sacred Head, Now Wounded"
"Thou Art Worthy"

We Listen to the Word of God

First Reader: A reading from 2 Chronicles:

"Now in the first years of Cyrus king of Persia, that the word of the LORD spoken by the mouth of Jeremiah might be fulfilled, the LORD stirred up the spirit of Cyrus king of Persia, so that he made a proclamation throughout all his kingdom, and also put it in writing, saying, 'Thus says Cyrus king of Persia: "All the kingdoms of the earth the LORD God of heaven has given me. And He has commanded me to build Him a house at Jerusalem which is in Judah. Who is there among you of all His people? May the LORD his God be with him, and let him go up!"'" (36:22–23).

This is the word of the Lord.

Response: Thanks be to God.

Second Reader: A reading from the gospel of John:

"And as Moses lifted up the serpent in the wilderness, even so must the Son of Man be lifted up, that whoever believes in him should not perish but have eternal life. For God so loved the world that he gave His only begotten Son, that whoever believes in Him should not perish but have everlasting life. For God did not send His Son into the world to condemn the world, but that the world through Him might be saved. He who believes in Him is not condemned; but he who does not believe is condemned already, because he has not believed in the name of the only begotten Son of God. And this is the condemnation, that the light has come into the world, and men loved darkness rather than light, because their deeds were evil. For everyone practicing evil hates the light and does not come to the light, lest his deeds should be exposed. But he who does the truth comes to the light, that his deeds may be clearly seen, that they have been done in God" (3:14–21).

This is the word of the Lord.

Response: Thanks be to God.

We Respond to the Word of God

Question: Why do we emphasize the new birth during Lent?

Answer: Even though Lent is primarily an identification with Jesus in His death, the death is never to be separated from the resurrection. Jesus died, not to remain dead, but to conquer death and rise to new life.

Question: What does that have to do with us?

Answer: During Lent we die to our sin so that we may rise with Christ.

Question: So the emphasis on the new birth is not at odds with Lent?

Answer: No, quite the contrary. Lent more than any other season points to our baptism into Christ which Paul describes as a baptism into His death and resurrection. "Therefore we were buried with Him through baptism into death, that just as Christ was raised from the dead by the glory of the Father, even so we also should walk in newness of life" (Rom. 6:4).

The Prayer of Response

Leader: Let us pray.

Lord, we were glad when we went up into the
house of the Lord,
When our feet stood within Your gates.
We pray for the peace of Jerusalem
And of the world.
May they prosper who love You.
May Peace be within their walls;
May they prosper who seek after You.
Amen.

(Adaptation of Ps. 122)

We Are Sent Forth

Leader: God, who is rich in mercy, because of the
great love with which He loved us, even when
we were dead in sin, made us alive with Christ.

Response: Thanks be to God.

FIFTH WEEK IN LENT

We Prepare to Worship God

Leader: Dear family, we are now coming closer to the
time of our Lord's death. During Lent we have
experienced the gradual revelation of our
Lord's mission. In His baptism He is revealed
as God's Son; at the Temptation we experience His power over Satan; in the temple

prophecy, a foreshadowing of His resurrection; in His words to Nicodemus, a savior; and now, our Lord reveals His mission of death.

Let us pray.

Father, in Your love for the world You sent Your only begotten Son to suffer as one of us and to die in our place. Save us by His work, inspire us through His love, and guide us by His example, who lives and reigns with You and the Holy Spirit, one God, forever and ever. Amen.

Hymn: *Sing one of the following hymns:*
"I Smite upon My Troubled Breast"
"In the Cross of Christ I Glory"
"He Was Wounded for Our Transgressions"

We Listen to the Word of God

First   A reading from Jeremiah:
Reader: " 'Behold, the days are coming,' says the LORD, 'when I will make a new covenant with the house of Israel and with the house of Judah— not according to the covenant that I made with their fathers in the day that I took them by the hand to bring them out of the land of Egypt, My covenant which they broke, though I was a husband to them,' says the LORD. 'But this is the covenant that I will make with the house of Israel: After those days, says the LORD, I will put My law in their minds, and write it on their hearts; and I will be their God, and they shall be My people.

No more shall every man teach his neighbor, and every man his brother, saying, "Know the LORD," for they all shall know Me, from the least of them to the greatest of them,' says the LORD" (31:31–34).

This is the word of the Lord.

Response: Thanks be to God.

Second Reader: A reading from the gospel according to John: "Now there were certain Greeks among those who came up to worship at the feast. Then they came to Philip, who was from Bethsaida of Galilee, and asked him, saying, 'Sir, we wish to see Jesus.' Philip came and told Andrew, and in turn Andrew and Philip told Jesus. But Jesus answered them, saying, 'The hour has come that the Son of Man should be glorified. Most assuredly, I say to you, unless a grain of wheat falls into the ground and dies, it remains alone; but if it dies, it produces much grain. He who loves his life will lose it, and he who hates his life in this world will keep it for eternal life. If anyone serves Me, let him follow Me; and where I am, there My servant will be also. If anyone serves Me, him My Father will honor. Now My soul is troubled, and what shall I say? "Father, save Me from this hour"? But for this purpose I came to this hour. Father, glorify Your name.' Then a voice came from heaven, saying, 'I have both glorified it and will glorify it again.' Therefore the people who stood by and heard it said that it had thundered. Others said, 'An angel has spoken to Him.' Jesus answered and said, 'This voice did not come because of Me, but for your sake. Now is the judgment of this world; now the ruler of this world will be cast out. And I, if I am lifted up from the earth, will draw all peoples to Myself.' This He said, signifying by what death He would die" (12:20–33).

This is the word of the Lord.

Response: Thanks be to God.

We Respond to the Word of God

The Inquiry and Instruction

Question: What should we meditate on this week?

Answer: The heart of our meditation this week is the verse from the Gospel reading: "Unless a grain of wheat falls into the ground and dies, it remains alone; but if it dies, it produces much grain" (John 12:24).

Question: What does it mean?

Answer: It is a reference to the death of Christ. He is the grain of wheat that dies and produces much fruit.

Question: What kind of response should I have?

Answer: Jesus said, "He who loves his life will lose it, and he who hates his life in this world will keep it for eternal life" (John 12:25).

The Prayer of Response

Leader: Let us pray.

Lord, create in us a clean heart
And renew a steadfast spirit within us.
Do not cast us away from Your presence,
And do not take Your Holy Spirit from us.
Restore to us the joy of Your salvation,
And uphold us with Your generous Spirit,
O Lord, open our lips,
And our mouth shall show forth Your praise.
Amen.

(Adaptation of Ps. 51:10–12, 15)

We Are Sent Forth

Leader: "The hour has come that the Son of Man should be glorified" (John 12:23).

Response: Thanks be to God.

HOLY WEEK

HOLY WEEK The circle represents wholeness and is also the ancient motif for eternity. Inside are familiar symbols. The design draws the worshiper into the center of the whole, thus underscoring Christ's central role in all things, temporal and eternal.

INTRODUCTION TO
Holy Week

In the Western church Holy Week is not a season to itself; it is part of Lent. But, because it is an intensification of Lent and the most solemn week of the Christian year, I have chosen to set it apart to accent its importance for the family.

The spiritual nature of Holy Week may be seen by the names given to it by various Christians. It has been called Major Week, Greater Week, Authentic Week, Week of Salvation, and Sorrowful and Mournful Week. A favorite designation used by many Christians is Passion Week, because it commemorates the events of the Passion.

The heart of Holy Week is the three-day commemoration (*Triduum*) which begins on Thursday evening and ends on Sunday. These three days constitute the heart of the church year, for during this time we move through the Last Supper, the denial by Judas, the prayer of our Lord in Gethsemane, His trial, crucifixion, burial, and resurrection.

In order to stress the importance of Holy Week, I have prepared family services for every day beginning with Palm Sunday. The purpose of these services is to take the family step by step through the last week of Christ's life on earth. But the point is not to provide an educational tool assisting the family in memorizing what Jesus did each day of His last week. Rather, the focus is on our journey and pilgrimage with Him.

How can we as a family actually enter into the passion of Christ? How can our spiritual pilgrimage be brought up into the passion of our Lord? How can we, with Him, experience the power of His death in our own life? The focus of each day, if taken seriously, will mesh the family pilgrimage with that of Jesus.

Sunday: The entrance into Jerusalem calls us into a preview of the whole week, for the Palm Sunday service moves from the joy of "Hosanna! Blessed is He who comes in the name of the LORD!" to the cry "Crucify Him!" (Mark 11:9; 15:13).

Monday: Mary's love for Jesus exhibited in the washing of His feet calls us into the commitment.

Tuesday: Christ calls us to faith in Him.

Wednesday: The focus is the betrayal of Judas.

Thursday: We begin the journey into His death as He is taken captive.

Friday: We are taken into His death.

Saturday: We are taken into His grave.

It should be noted that during Holy Week the Old Testament selections are drawn from the servant passages of Isaiah, culminating in the greatest of them, Isaiah 53. In keeping with the severity of the season the services are more plain. There is no singing, no inquiry and instruction, and there are relatively few responses. The feeling is one of sobriety that leads to pensive meditation on the death of our Lord.

The most ancient custom during Holy Week falls in the three-day period between Thursday evening and Sunday morning. These are the three most sober days of the Christian experience. In order to help your family identify with Christ's suffering and prepare for the resurrection, I suggest you do three things together as a family:

(1) Worship together at church. Since this should not be a party time, a time to frolic or play, it may be made more serious by attendance at church services, more strict adherence to fasting, and periods of silence. Many churches have Maundy evening service on Thursday, noon service from 12:00 P.M. to 3:00 P.M. on Friday, and veneration of the cross service on Friday evening. Go to all or as many of these services as possible.

(2) During this time eat simply or perhaps not at all. Let the experience of Christ's death be felt in the stomach. Children should not totally abstain from food, but adults may choose not to eat.

(3) Observe periods of silence on both Friday and Saturday. Turn off the radio and TV, take the phone off the hook if possible, and spend blocks of time in absolute silence, prayer, and meditation. These disciplines will help you and your family to prepare for the festive joy that will come later in the resurrection celebration.

PALM SUNDAY

We Prepare to Worship

Leader: Today is Palm Sunday. On this day we celebrate the entrance of Christ into Jerusalem, a most joyous occasion. We also anticipate His passion and death, a time that brings us great sorrow. Our family service will reflect both of these moods.

Let us pray.

Lord Jesus, You who were hailed as king on this day and crucified a few days afterward, grant us entrance into Your passion, that we may participate in Your resurrection, through You, our Lord. Amen.

Hymn: *Sing one of the following hymns:*
"All Glory, Laud, and Honor"
"Bless His Holy Name"

Before the reading of the Scriptures, appoint the following readers: Narrator, Jesus, Judas, Crowd, High Priest, Girl, Peter, Pilate, Soldiers,

Chief Priests, Centurion. Have the family gather around the one holding this book.

We Listen to the Word of God

Reader: A reading about the entrance of Christ into Jerusalem on Palm Sunday:
"They brought the colt to Jesus and threw their garments on it, and He sat on it. And many spread their garments on the road, and others cut down leafy branches from the trees and spread them on the road. Then those who went before and those who followed cried out, saying:
'Hosanna!
"Blessed is He who comes in the name of the LORD!"
Blessed is the kingdom of our father David
That comes in the name of the Lord!
Hosanna in the highest!'" (Mark 11:7–10).

This is the word of the Lord.

Response: Thanks be to God.

We Respond to the Word of God

Leader: It has been a custom in the church to read the passion of our Lord Jesus Christ on Palm Sunday. Through this reading we prepare for the most solemn events of this week.

Narrator: "Then they came to a place which was named Gethsemane; and He said to His disciples,

Jesus: 'Sit here while I pray.'

Narrator: And He took Peter, James, and John with Him, and He began to be troubled and deeply distressed. Then He said to them:

Jesus: 'My soul is exceedingly sorrowful, even to death. Stay here and watch.'

Narrator: He went a little farther, and fell on the ground, and prayed that if it were possible, the hour might pass from Him. And He said,

Jesus: 'Abba, Father, all things are possible for You. Take this cup away from Me; nevertheless, not what I will, but what You will.'

Narrator: Then He came and found them sleeping, and said to Peter,

Jesus: 'Simon, are you sleeping? Could you not watch one hour? Watch and pray, lest you enter into temptation. The spirit truly is ready, but the flesh is weak.'

Narrator: Again He went away and prayed, and spoke the same words. And when He returned, He found them asleep again, for their eyes were heavy; and they did not know what to answer Him. Then He came the third time and said to them,

Jesus: 'Are you still sleeping and resting? It is enough! The hour has come; behold, the Son of Man is being betrayed into the hands of sinners. Rise up, let us go. See, My betrayer is at hand.'

Narrator: And immediately, while He was still speaking, Judas, one of the twelve, with a great multitude with swords and clubs, came from the chief priests and the scribes and the elders. Now His betrayer had given them a signal, saying,

Judas: 'Whomever I kiss, He is the One; take Him and lead Him away safely.'

Narrator: And as soon as He had come, immediately he went up to Him and said to Him,

Judas: 'Rabbi, Rabbi!'

Narrator: And kissed Him. Then they laid their hands on Him and took Him. And one of those who stood by drew his sword and struck the servant of the high priest, and cut off his ear. Then Jesus answered and said to them,

Jesus: 'Have you come out, as against a robber, with swords and clubs to take Me? I was daily with you in the temple teaching, and you did not take Me. But the Scriptures must be fulfilled.'

Narrator: Then they all forsook Him and fled. Now a certain young man followed Him, having a linen cloth thrown around his naked body. And the young men laid hold of him. And he left the linen cloth and fled from them naked. And they led Jesus away to the high priest; and with him were assembled all the chief priests, the elders, and the scribes. But Peter followed Him at a distance, right into the courtyard of the high priest. And he sat with the servants and warmed himself at the fire.

And the chief priests and all the council sought testimony against Jesus to put Him to death, and found none. For many bore false witness against Him, but their testimonies did not agree. And some rose up and bore false witness against Him, saying,

Crowd: 'We heard Him say, "I will destroy this temple that is made with hands, and within three days I will build another made without hands."'

Narrator: But not even then did their testimony agree. And the high priest stood up in the midst and asked Jesus, saying,

Priest: 'Do You answer nothing? What is it these men testify against You?'

Narrator: But He kept silent and answered nothing. Again the high priest asked Him, saying to Him,

Priest: 'Are You the Christ, the Son of the Blessed?'

Narrator: And Jesus said,

Jesus: 'I am. And you will see the Son of Man sitting at the right hand of the Power, and coming with the clouds of heaven.'

Narrator: The high priest tore his clothes and said,

Priest: 'What further need do we have of witnesses? You have heard the blasphemy! What do you think?'

Narrator: And they all condemned Him to be worthy of

death. Then some began to spit on Him, and to blindfold Him, and to beat Him, and to say to Him,

Crowd: 'Prophesy!'

Narrator: And the officers struck Him with the palms of their hands. Now as Peter was below in the courtyard, one of the servant girls of the high priest came. And when she saw Peter warming himself, she looked at him and said,

Girl: 'You also were with Jesus of Nazareth.'

Narrator: But he denied it, saying,

Peter: 'I neither know nor understand what you are saying.' And he went out on the porch, and a rooster crowed. And the servant girl saw him again, and began to say to those who stood by,

Girl: 'This is one of them.'

Narrator: But he denied it again. And a little later those who stood by said to Peter again.

Girl: 'Surely you are one of them; for you are a Galilean, and your speech shows it.'

Narrator: But he began to curse and swear.

Peter: 'I do not know this Man of whom you speak!'

Narrator: And a second time the rooster crowed. And Peter called to mind the word that Jesus had said to him,

Jesus: 'Before the rooster crows twice, you will deny Me three times.'

Narrator: And when he thought about it, he wept. Immediately, in the morning, the chief priests held a consultation with the elders and scribes and the whole council; and they bound Jesus, led Him away, and delivered Him to Pilate. Then Pilate asked Him,

Pilate: 'Are You the King of the Jews?'

Narrator: And He answered and said to him,

Jesus: 'It is as you say.'

Narrator: Then Pilate asked Him again, saying,

Pilate: 'Do You answer nothing? See how many things they testify against You!'

Narrator: But Jesus still answered nothing, so that Pilate marveled. Now at the feast he was accustomed to releasing one prisoner to them, whomever they requested. And there was one named Barabbas, who was chained with his fellow insurrectionists; they had committed murder in the insurrection. Then the multitude, crying aloud, began to ask him to do just as he had always done for them. But Pilate answered them, saying,

Pilate: 'Do you want me to release to you the King of Jews?'

Narrator: For he knew that the chief priests had handed Him over because of envy. But the chief priests stirred up the crowd, so that he should rather release Barabbas to them. And Pilate answered and said to them again,

Pilate: 'What then do you want me to do with Him whom you call the King of the Jews?'

Narrator: So they cried out again,

Crowd: 'Crucify Him!'

Narrator: Then Pilate said to them,

Pilate: 'Why, what evil has He done?'

Narrator: And they cried out more exceedingly,

Crowd: 'Crucify Him!'

Narrator: So Pilate, wanting to gratify the crowd, released Barabbas to them; and he delivered Jesus, after he had scourged Him, to be crucified. Then the soldiers led Him away into the hall called Praetorium, and they called together the whole garrison. And they clothed Him with purple; and they twisted a crown of thorns, put it on His head, and began to salute Him,

Soldiers: 'Hail, King of the Jews!'

Narrator: Then they struck Him on the head with a reed and spat on Him; and bowing the knee, they worshiped Him. And when they had mocked Him, they took the purple off Him, put His own clothes on Him, and led Him out to crucify Him. Now they compelled a certain man, Simon a Cyrenian, the father of Alexander and Rufus, as he was coming out of the country and passing by, to bear His cross. And they brought Him to the place Golgotha, which is translated, Place of a Skull. Then they gave Him wine mingled with myrrh to drink, but He did not take it. And when they crucified Him, they divided His garments, casting lots for them to determine what every man should take. Now it was the third hour, and they crucified Him. And the inscription of His accusation was written above: THE KING OF THE JEWS. With Him they also crucified two robbers, one on His right and the other on His left. So the Scripture was fulfilled which says, 'And He was numbered with the transgressors.' And those who passed by blasphemed Him, wagging their heads and saying, 'Aha! You who destroy the temple and build it in three days, save Yourself, and come down from the cross!' Likewise the chief priests also, together with the scribes, mocked and said among themselves,

Chief Priests: 'He saved others; Himself He cannot save. Let the Christ, the King of Israel, descend now from the cross, that we may see and believe.'

Narrator: And those who were crucified with Him reviled Him. Now when the sixth hour had come, there was darkness over the whole land until the ninth hour. And at the ninth hour Jesus cried out with a loud voice, saying,

Jesus: 'Eloi, Eloi, lama sabachthani?'

Narrator: Which is translated, 'My God, My God, why have You forsaken Me?' Some of those who stood by, when they heard it, said,

Crowd: 'Look. He is calling for Elijah!'

Narrator: Then someone ran and filled a sponge full of sour wine, put it on a reed, and offered it to Him to drink, saying,

Soldier: 'Let Him alone; let us see if Elijah will come to take Him down.'

Narrator: And Jesus cried out with a loud voice, and breathed His last. Then the veil of the temple was torn in two from top to bottom. Now when the centurion, who stood opposite Him, saw that He cried out like this and breathed His last, he said,

Centurion: 'Truly this Man was the Son of God!'

Narrator: There were also women looking on from afar, among whom were Mary Magdalene, Mary the mother of James the Less and of Joses, and Salome, who also followed Him and ministered to Him when He was in Galilee; and many other women who came up with Him to Jerusalem. Now when evening had come, because it was the Preparation Day, that is, the day before the Sabbath, Joseph of Arimathea, a prominent council member, who was himself waiting for the kingdom of God, coming and taking courage, went in to Pilate and asked for the body of Jesus. Pilate marveled that He was already dead; and summoning the centurion, he asked him if He had been dead for some time. And when he found out from the centurion, he granted the body to Joseph.

Then he bought fine linen, took Him down, and wrapped Him in the linen. And he laid Him in a tomb which had been hewn out of the rock, and rolled a stone against the door of the tomb. And Mary Magdalene and Mary the mother of Joses observed where He was laid" (Mark 14:32–72; 15:1–47).

Leader: Let us pray.

Most merciful God, we give You grateful thanks that Your Son has been highly exalted and given a name which is above every name, that at the name of Jesus every knee should bow, of those in heaven, and of those on earth, and that every tongue should confess that Jesus Christ is Lord, to the glory of God the Father. Amen.

(Adaptation of Phil. 2:5–11)

Response: Thanks be to God.

MONDAY IN HOLY WEEK

Leader: This is the last Monday before the death of our Lord. It is a solemn and holy day, one in which we are called to remember Him. What does the church remember on Monday of Holy Week? The servant portrayal of Christ prophesied by Isaiah.

Reader: A reading from Isaiah:
"'Behold! My Servant whom I uphold,
My Elect One in whom My soul delights!
I have put My Spirit upon Him;
He will bring forth justice to the Gentiles.
He will not cry out, nor raise His voice,
Nor cause His voice to be heard in the street.
A bruised reed He will not break
And smoking flax He will not quench;
He will bring forth justice for truth.
He will not fail nor be discouraged,
Till He has established justice in the earth;
And the coastlands shall wait for his law.'
Thus says God the LORD,
Who created the heavens and stretched them
        out,
Who spread forth the earth and that which
        comes from it,
Who gives breath to the people on it,
And spirit to those who walk on it:
'I, the LORD, have called You in
        righteousness,
And will hold Your hand;
I will keep You and give You as a covenant to
        the people,
As a light to the Gentiles,
To open blind eyes,
To bring out prisoners from the prison,
Those who sit in darkness from the prison
        house.
I am the LORD, that is My name;
And My glory I will not give to another,
Nor My praise to graven images.

Behold, the former things have come to pass,
And new things I declare;
Before they spring forth
I tell you of them'" (Isa. 42:1–9).

Here ends the lesson. (*A short period of silence shall be kept.*)

Leader: What event in the life of Jesus do we recall on Monday of Holy Week? We recall Mary, the sister of Martha, who washed Jesus' feet with fragrant oil.

Reader: A reading from the gospel of John:
"Then, six days before the Passover, Jesus came to Bethany, where Lazarus was who had been dead, whom He had raised from the dead. There they made Him a supper; and Martha served, but Lazarus was one of those who sat at the table with Him. Then Mary took a pound of very costly oil of spikenard, anointed the feet of Jesus, and wiped His feet with her hair. And the house was filled with the fragrance of the oil. Then one of His disciples, Judas Iscariot, Simon's son, who would betray Him, said, 'Why was this fragrant oil not sold for three hundred denarii and given to the poor?' This he said, not that he cared for the poor, but because he was a thief, and had the money box; and he used to take what was put in it. Then Jesus said, 'Let her alone; she has kept this for the day of My burial. For the poor you have with you always, but Me you do not have always.' Then a great many of

Jews knew that He was there; and they came, not for Jesus' sake only, but that they might also see Lazarus, whom He had raised from the dead. But the chief priests took counsel that they might also put Lazarus to death, because on account of him many of the Jews went away and believed in Jesus" (12:1–11).

Here ends the reading. (*A short period of silence shall be kept.*)

Leader: Let us pray.

Lord God, cause that we should lay aside every weight, and the sin which so easily ensnares us, and run with endurance the race that is set before us. May we look to Jesus, the author and finisher of our faith, who for the joy that was set before Him, endured the cross, despised the shame, and has sat down at the right hand of the throne of God.

(Adaptation of Heb. 12:1–3)

Response: Thanks be to God.

TUESDAY IN HOLY WEEK

Leader: My dear family, this is the last Tuesday before our Lord's death. It is a solemn and holy day, one in which we are called to remember Him. On Tuesday of Holy Week we remember a second servant portrayal of Christ prophesied by Isaiah.

Reader: A reading from Isaiah:
"Listen, O coastlands, to Me,
And take heed, you peoples from afar!
The LORD has called Me from the womb;
From the matrix of My mother
He has made mention of My name.
And He has made My mouth like a sharp
     sword;
In the shadow of His hand He has hidden Me,
And made Me a polished shaft;
In His quiver He has hidden Me.
And He said to me,
'You are My servant, O Israel,
In whom I will be glorified.'
Then I said, 'I have labored in vain,
I have spent my strength for nothing and in
     vain;
Yet surely my just reward is with the LORD,
And my work with my God.'
And now the LORD says,
Who formed Me from the womb to be His
     Servant,
To bring Jacob back to Him,
So that Israel is gathered to Him
(For I shall be glorious in the eyes of the LORD,
And My God shall be My strength),
Indeed He says,
'It is too small a thing that You should be My
     Servant
To raise up the tribes of Jacob,
And to restore the preserved ones of Israel;
I will give You as a light to the Gentiles.

That You should be My salvation to the ends of the earth'" (49:1–6).

Here ends the reading. (*A short period of silence shall be kept.*)

Leader: What event from the life of Jesus do we recall on Tuesday of Holy Week? We recall Jesus' cry for the people to believe in Him.

Reader: A reading from the gospel of John:
"But although He had done so many signs before them, they did not believe in Him, that the word of Isaiah the prophet might be fulfilled, which he spoke:
'Lord, who has believed our report? And to whom has the arm of the LORD been revealed?' . . .
For they loved the praise of men more than the praise of God. Then Jesus cried out and said, 'He who believes in Me, believes not in Me but in Him who sent Me. And he who sees Me sees Him who sent Me. I have come as a light into the world, that whoever believes in Me should not abide in darkness. And if anyone hears My words and does not believe, I do not judge him; for I did not come to judge the world but to save the world. He who rejects Me, and does not receive My words, has that which judges him—the word that I have spoken will judge him in the last day. For I have not spoken on My own authority; but the Father who sent Me gave Me a command, what I should say and what I

should speak. And I know that His command is everlasting life. Therefore, whatever I speak, just as the Father has told Me, so I speak'" (12:37–38; 43–50).

Here end the words of Jesus. (*A short period of silence shall be kept.*)

Leader: Let us pray.

Father, the message of the cross is foolishness to those who are perishing, but to us who are being saved it is the power of God. O Lord, cause us not to glory in the wisdom of men, but in Christ Jesus, who became for us the wisdom from God—and righteousness, and sanctification, and redemption.

(Adaptation of 1 Cor. 1:18–31)

Response: Thanks be to God.

WEDNESDAY IN HOLY WEEK

Leader: This is the last Wednesday before the end of our Lord's ministry on earth. It is a solemn and holy day, one in which we are called to remember Him. On Wednesday of Holy Week we remember a third servant portrayal of Christ prophesied by Isaiah.

Reader: A reading from Isaiah:
"The Lord GOD has given Me
The tongue of the learned,

That I should know how to speak
A word in season to him who is weary.
He awakens Me morning by morning,
He awakens My ear
To hear as the learned.
The Lord GOD has opened My ear;
And I was not rebellious,
Nor did I turn away.
I gave My back to those who struck Me,
And My cheeks to those who plucked out the
        beard;
I did not hide My face from shame and spit-
        ting.
For the Lord GOD will help Me;
Therefore I will not be disgraced:
Therefore I have set My face like a flint,
And I know that I will not be ashamed.
He is near who justifies Me;
Who will contend with Me?
Let us stand together.
Who is My adversary?
Let him come near Me.
Surely the Lord GOD will help me;
Who is he who will condemn Me?" (50:4–9).

Here ends the reading. (A *short period of silence shall be kept.*)

Leader: What event from the life of Jesus do we recall
on the Wednesday of Holy Week? The identification of Judas as the betrayer.

Reader: A reading from the gospel of John:
"When Jesus had said these things, He was

158

troubled in spirit, and testified and said, 'Most assuredly, I say to you, one of you will betray Me.' Then the disciples looked at one another, perplexed about whom He spoke. Now there was leaning on Jesus' bosom one of His disciples, whom Jesus loved. Simon Peter therefore motioned to him to ask who it was of whom He spoke. Then, leaning back on Jesus' breast, he said to Him, 'Lord, who is it?' Jesus answered, 'It is he to whom I shall give a piece of bread when I have dipped it.' And having dipped the bread, He gave it to Judas Iscariot, the son of Simon. Now after the piece of bread, Satan entered him. Then Jesus said to him, 'What you do, do quickly.' But no one at the table knew for what reason He said this to him. For some thought, because Judas had the money box, that Jesus had said to him, 'Buy those things we need for the feast,' or that he should give something to the poor. Having received the piece of bread, he then went out immediately. And it was night. So, when he had gone out, Jesus said, 'Now the Son of Man is glorified, and God is glorified in Him. If God is glorified in Him, God will also glorify Him in Himself, and glorify Him immediately. Little children, I shall be with you a little while longer. You will seek Me; and as I said to the Jews, "Where I am going, you cannot come," so now I say to you. A new commandment I give to you, that you love one another; as I have loved you, that you also love one another. By this all will know that you are My disciples, if you have love for one another'" (13:21–35).

Here ends the lesson. (*A short period of silence shall be kept.*)

Leader: Let us pray.

Father, we bless You for Your Son, who came at the end of the ages to put away sin by the sacrifice of Himself. May we who believe in Him eagerly wait for the salvation He brings when He comes the second time, through Christ our Lord. Amen.

(Adaptation of Heb. 9:26, 28)

Response: Thanks be to God.

THURSDAY IN HOLY WEEK

Leader: Thursday in Holy Week is a most solemn day because it marks the beginning of the end. On Thursday of Holy Week we remember the preparation Israel made for its flight from Egypt.

Reader: A reading from Exodus:
"Now the LORD spoke to Moses and Aaron in the land of Egypt, saying, 'This month shall be your beginning of months; it shall be the first month of the year to you. Speak to all the congregation of Israel, saying: "On the tenth

day of this month every man shall take for himself a lamb, according to the house of his father, a lamb for a household. And if the household is too small for the lamb, let him and his neighbor next to his house take it according to the number of persons; according to each man's need you shall make your count for the lamb. Your lamb shall be without blemish, a male of the first year. You may take it from the sheep or from the goats. Now you shall keep it until the fourteenth day of the same month. Then the whole assembly of the congregation of Israel shall kill it at twilight. And they shall take some of the blood and put it on the two doorposts and on the lintel of the houses where they eat it. Then they shall eat the flesh on that night; roasted in fire, with unleavened bread and with bitter herbs they shall eat it. Do not eat it raw, nor boiled at all with water, but roasted in fire—its head with its legs and its entrails. You shall let none of it remain until morning, and what remains of it until morning you shall burn with fire. And thus you shall eat it: with a belt on your waist, your sandals on your feet, and your staff in your hand. So you shall eat it in haste. It is the LORD'S Passover. For I will pass through the land of Egypt on that night, and will strike all the firstborn in the land of Egypt, both man and beast; and against all the gods of Egypt I will execute judgment: I am the LORD. Now the blood shall be a sign for you on the houses where you are. And

when I see the blood, I will pass over you; and
the plague shall not be on you to destroy you
when I strike the land of Egypt. So this day
shall be to you a memorial; and you shall keep
it as a feast to the LORD throughout your generations"'" (12:1–14).

Here ends the lesson. (*A short time of silence
shall be kept.*)

Leader: From the life of Jesus, we recall on Thursday
of Holy Week the Last Supper and the wash-
ing of the disciples' feet.

Reader: A reading from the gospel of John:
"Now before the feast of the Passover, when
Jesus knew that His hour had come that He
should depart from this world to the Father,
having loved His own who were in the world,
He loved them to the end. And supper being
ended, the devil having already put it into the
heart of Judas Iscariot, Simon's son, to betray
Him, Jesus, knowing that the Father had
given all things into His hands, and that He
had come from God and was going to God,
rose from supper and laid aside His garments,
took a towel and girded Himself. After that,
He poured water into a basin and began to
wash the disciples' feet, and to wipe them
with the towel with which He was girded.
Then He came to Simon Peter. And Peter said
to Him, 'Lord, are You washing my feet?' Jesus
answered and said to him, 'What I am doing
you do not understand now, but you will know

after this.' Peter said to Him, 'You shall never wash my feet!' Jesus answered him, 'If I do not wash you, you have no part with Me.' Simon Peter said to Him, 'Lord, not my feet only, but also my hands and my head!' Jesus said to him, 'He who is bathed needs only to wash his feet, but is completely clean; and you are clean, but not all of you.' For He knew who would betray Him; therefore He said, 'You are not all clean.' So when He had washed their feet, taken His garments, and sat down again, He said to them, 'Do you know what I have done to you? You call me Teacher and Lord, and you say well, for so I am. If I then, your Lord and Teacher, have washed your feet, you also ought to wash one another's feet. For I have given you an example, that you should do as I have done to you'" (13:1–15).

Here ends the lesson. (*A short period of silence shall be kept.*)

Leader: Let us pray.

Lord, we bless You for the bread and the cup which You have given as signs of Your presence. May we who eat and drink at Your table show forth Your death till You come. Amen.

Response: Thanks be to God.

GOOD FRIDAY

Leader: This day is most holy, for on this day our Lord Jesus gave over His life for the salvation of the world. Hear the word of the Lord as spoken by Isaiah.

First Reader: A reading from Isaiah:

"Behold, My Servant shall deal prudently,
He shall be exalted and extolled and be very
    high.
Just as many were astonished at you,
So His visage was marred more than any man,
And His form more than the sons of men;
So shall He sprinkle many nations.
Kings shall shut their mouths at Him;
For what had not been told them they shall
    see,
And what they had not heard they shall
    consider.
Who has believed our report?
And to whom has the arm of the
    LORD been revealed?
For He shall grow up before Him as a tender
    plant,
And as a root out of dry ground.
He has no form or comeliness;
And when we see Him,
There is no beauty that we should desire Him.
He is despised and rejected by men,
A man of sorrows and acquainted with grief.

And we hid, as it were, our faces from Him;
He was despised, and we did not esteem Him.
Surely He has borne our griefs
And carried our sorrows;
Yet we esteemed Him stricken,
Smitten by God, and afflicted.
But He was wounded for our transgressions,
He was bruised for our iniquities;
The chastisement for our peace was upon
    Him,
And by His stripes we are healed.
All we like sheep have gone astray;
We have turned, every one, to his own way;
And the LORD has laid on Him the iniquity of
    us all.
He was oppressed and He was afflicted,
Yet he opened not His mouth;
He was led as a lamb to the slaughter,
And as a sheep before its shearers is silent,
So He opened not His mouth.
He was taken from prison and from judgment,
And who will declare His generation?
For He was cut off from the land of the living;
For the transgressions of My people He was
    stricken.
And they made His grave with the wicked—
But with the rich at His death,
Because He had done no violence,
Nor was any deceit in His mouth.
Yet it pleased the LORD to bruise Him;
He has put Him to grief.
When you make His soul an offering for sin,

He shall see His seed, He shall prolong His
days,
And the pleasure of the Lord shall prosper in
His hand.
He shall see the travail of His soul, and be
satisfied.
By His knowledge My righteous Servant shall
justify many,
For He shall bear their iniquities.
Therefore I will divide Him a portion with
the great,
And He shall divide the spoil with the strong,
Because He poured out His soul unto death,
And He was numbered with the transgressors,
And He bore the sin of many,
And made intercession for the transgressors"
(52:13–15; 53:1–12).

Here ends the lesson. (*A short time of silence
shall be kept.*)

Leader: Hear the account of our Savior's death.

Second   "So then Pilate took Jesus and scourged Him.
Reader: And the soldiers twisted a crown of thorns
and put it on His head, and they put on Him a
purple robe. Then they said, 'Hail, King of
the Jews!' And they struck Him with their
hands. Pilate then went out again, and said to
them, 'Behold, I am bringing Him out to you,
that you may know that I find no fault in
Him.' Then Jesus came out, wearing the
crown of thorns and the purple robe. And Pilate said to them, 'Behold the Man!' There-

fore, when the chief priests and officers saw Him, they cried out, saying, 'Crucify Him, crucify Him!' Pilate said to them, 'You take Him and crucify Him, for I find no fault in Him.' The Jews answered him, 'We have a law, and according to our law He ought to die, because He made Himself the Son of God.' Therefore, when Pilate heard that saying, he was the more afraid, and went again into the Praetorium, and said to Jesus, 'Where are You from?' But Jesus gave him no answer. Then Pilate said to Him, 'Are You not speaking to me? Do You not know that I have power to crucify You, and power to release You?' Jesus answered, 'You could have no power at all against Me unless it had been given you from above. Therefore the one who delivered Me to you has the greater sin.' From then on Pilate sought to release Him, but the Jews cried out, saying, 'If you let this Man go, you are not Caesar's friend. Whoever makes himself a king speaks against Caesar.' When Pilate therefore heard that saying, he brought Jesus out and sat down on the judgment seat in a place that is called The Pavement, but in Hebrew, Gabbatha. Now it was the Preparation Day of the Passover, and about the sixth hour. And he said to the Jews, 'Behold your King!' But they cried out, 'Away with Him, away with Him! Crucify Him!' Pilate said to them, 'Shall I crucify your King?' The chief priests answered, 'We have no king but Caesar!' So he delivered Him to them to be crucified. So they took Jesus and led Him away. And He, bearing His cross, went out to a place called the Place of a Skull, which is called in Hebrew, Golgotha, where they crucified Him, and two others with Him, one on either side, and Jesus in the center. Now Pilate wrote a title and put it on the cross. And the writing was: JESUS OF NAZARETH/ THE KING OF THE JEWS. Then many of the Jews read this title, for the place where Jesus was crucified was near the city; and it was written in Hebrew, Greek, and Latin. Then the chief priests of the Jews said to Pilate, 'Do not write, "The King of the Jews," but "He said, 'I am the King of the Jews.'"' Pilate answered, 'What I have written, I have written.' Then the soldiers, when they had crucified Jesus, took His garments and made four parts, to each soldier a part, and also the tunic. Now the tunic was without seam, woven from the top in one piece. They said therefore among themselves, 'Let us not tear it, but cast lots for it, whose it shall be,' that the Scripture might be fulfilled which says: 'They divided My garments among them, / And for My clothing they cast lots.' Therefore the soldiers did these things. Now there stood by the cross of Jesus His mother and His mother's sister, Mary the wife of Clopas, and Mary Magdalene. When Jesus therefore saw His mother, and the disciple whom He loved standing by, He said to His mother, 'Woman, behold your son!' Then He said to the disci-

ple, 'Behold your mother!' And from that
hour the disciple took her to his own home.
After this, Jesus, knowing that all things were
now accomplished, that the Scripture might
be fulfilled, said, 'I thirst!' Now a vessel full of
sour wine was sitting there; and they filled a
sponge with sour wine, put it on a hyssop, and
put it to His mouth. So when Jesus had received the sour wine, He said, 'It is finished!'
And bowing His head, He gave up His spirit.
Therefore, because it was the Preparation
Day, that the bodies should not remain on the
cross on the Sabbath (for that Sabbath was a
high day), the Jews asked Pilate that their legs
might be broken, and that they might be
taken away. Then the soldiers came and broke
the legs of the first and of the other who was
crucified with Him. But when they came to
Jesus and saw that He was already dead, they
did not break his legs. But one of the soldiers
pierced His side with a spear, and immediately
blood and water came out. And he who has
seen has testified, and his testimony is true;
and he knows that he is telling the truth, so
that you may believe. For these things were
done that the Scripture should be fulfilled,
'Not one of His bones shall be broken.' And
again another Scripture says, 'They shall look
on Him whom they pierced'" (John 19:1–37).

Here ends the lesson. (*A short time of silence
shall be kept.*)

Leader: Let us pray.

Most merciful God, we bless You for a new and living way into Your presence. May we draw near with a true heart in full assurance of faith; may we hold fast the confession of our hope without wavering; may we consider how to stir up love and good works; may we not forsake the assembling of ourselves together; may we exhort one another as we see the day of Your return approaching, through Christ our Lord. Amen.

(Adaptation of Heb. 10:22–25)

Response: Thanks be to God.

SATURDAY IN HOLY WEEK

Leader: On this day of Holy Week our Lord's body lies in the grave. Hear the word of the Lord:

First Reader: "After this, Joseph of Arimathea, being a disciple of Jesus, but secretly, for fear of the Jews, asked Pilate that he might take away the body of Jesus; and Pilate gave him permission. So he came and took the body of Jesus. And Nicodemus, who at first came to Jesus by night, also came, bringing a mixture of myrrh and aloes, about a hundred pounds. Then they took the body of Jesus, and bound it in strips of linen with the spices, as the custom of the Jews is to bury. Now in the place where He was crucified there was a garden, and in the garden a new tomb in which no one had yet been laid. So there they laid Jesus, because of the Jews' Preparation Day, for the tomb was nearby" (John 19:38–42).

Here ends the lesson. *(A short period of silence shall be kept.)*

Second Reader: A reading from Psalm 31:
"In You, O LORD, I put my trust;
Let me never be ashamed;
Deliver me in Your righteousness.
Bow down Your ear to me,
Deliver me speedily;
Be my rock of refuge,
A fortress of defense to save me.
For You are my rock and my fortress;
Therefore, for Your name's sake,
Lead me and guide me.
Pull me out of the net which they have
    secretly laid for me,
For You are my strength.
Into Your hand I commit my spirit;
You have redeemed me,
    O LORD God of truth" (1–5).

Here ends the psalm. *(A short period of silence shall be kept.)*

Leader: Let us meditate on death through the words of Job:

Third Reader: "Man who is born of woman
Is of few days and full of trouble.
He comes forth like a flower and fades away;

171

He flees like a shadow and does not continue.
And do You open Your eyes on such a one,
And bring me to judgment with Yourself?
Who can bring a clean thing out of an
    unclean?
No one!
Since his days are determined,
The number of his months is with You,
You have appointed his limits, so that he
    cannot pass.
Look away from him that he may rest,
Till like a hired man he finishes his day.
For there is hope for a tree,
If it is cut down, that it will sprout again,
And that its tender shoots will not cease.
Though its roots may grow old in the earth,
And its stump may die in the ground,
Yet at the scent of water it will bud
And bring forth branches like a plant.
But man dies and is laid away;
Indeed he breathes his last
And where is he?
As water disappears from the sea,
And a river becomes parched and dries up,
So man lies down and does not rise.
Till the heavens are no more,
They will not awake
Nor be roused from their sleep.
Oh, that You would hide me in the grave, . . .
That You would appoint me a set time, and
    remember me!
If a man dies, shall he live again?" (14:1–14).

172

Here ends the reading. *(A short period of silence shall be kept.)*

Leader: Let us pray.

Lord, You are the judge to whom we must give account. Since the end of all things is at hand, teach us to be serious in conduct, watchful in prayer, and fervent in love, through Christ our Lord. Amen.

(Adapted from 1 Pet. 4:7–8)

Response: Thanks be to God.

EASTER AND PENTECOST

EASTER The Greek letters exclaim Christ's identity to worshipers. Greek was the universal language of the known world. Over and above, the cross dominates, suggesting the completed work of the cross and the resurrection of Christ.

AN INTRODUCTION
to *Easter and Pentecost*

In the church year Easter is not a single-day celebration, but an entire season. The season, taken from the Hebrew time between Passover and the Feast of Weeks, extends for fifty days to Pentecost. In the early church this was a special time—a time to extend the great joy of the resurrection and to celebrate the relationship of the newly baptized to the resurrected Lord. In terms of Christ's life, Easter particularly celebrates the presence of the risen Christ with His disciples and culminates in the Ascension and the sending of the Spirit on Pentecost.

On Easter the family returns to the more celebrative service of worship, a welcome change from the penitential Lenten season and the extremely somber services of Holy Week. The family begins with the most joyous and festive occasion, the feast of the resurrection on Easter Sunday. This service is designed for use at the family Easter meal.

The celebration continues for seven weeks. During the first week the family is called into belief, not as doubting Thomases who demand proof, but with the eye of faith;

in the second week Jesus becomes known to us in the breaking of the bread; during the third week Jesus is celebrated as the shepherd of the sheep; in the fourth week, He is presented as the way, the truth, and the life; in the fifth week, the promise of the coming of the Spirit links Jesus with the church and prepares us for His ascension, which we celebrate during the sixth week.

In the seventh and last week of Easter the family focuses in on the glory of Christ in His second coming, the expectation we now have since His ascension. Easter closes with Pentecost, the coming of the Spirit to a small community of God's people who were soon to spread the message of Christ around the world.

Family customs during Easter season all express the joy of the resurrection. The experience of Easter is the opposite of Lent, which accents sobriety. Easter is a joyous time, a time to have fun, laugh, play, picnic, and enjoy the outdoors. Develop a family Easter party, a special occasion to frolic because Christ is risen from the dead. Traditional symbols and customs of Easter include new clothes, an Easter parade, the Easter lamb cake, Easter eggs, the Easter bunny, Easter pastry, Easter ham, and Easter lilies. One should not fear using one or more of these ways to celebrate Easter, although it is always important to stress that these symbols serve the Easter spirit and are not ends in themselves. They remind us of Jesus' resurrection and point to the joy that is ours because Christ has conquered evil and has risen from the grave, symbolizing our new and eternal life.

(The dates for Easter, Ascension Day, and Pentecost are found in Appendix I.)

EASTER SUNDAY

We Prepare to Worship

Leader: *(Repeat three times.)*
Christ is risen!

Response: *(Repeat three times.)*
He is risen indeed!

Leader: People of God, this is the day when all who believe in Christ are delivered from the gloom of sin and restored to life eternal. This is the day when Christ broke the bonds of death and hell, and rose victorious from the grave. How glorious is this day when earth and heaven are joined. How blessed is this day when man and God are reconciled.

Let us pray.

Lord Jesus, You broke the bonds of death and hell and, on this day, rose victorious over the grave. O God, Your mercy and lovingkindness to us is wonderful and beyond our comprehension. May You, the Morning Star of creation, fill us with Your light and reign within us forever and ever. Amen.

Hymn: *Sing one of the following hymns:*
"Welcome, Happy Morning"
"This Is the Day That the Lord Hath Made"
"Because He Lives"

We Listen to the Word of God

First   A reading from Exodus:
Reader: "And when Pharaoh drew near, the children of Israel lifted their eyes, and behold, the Egyptians marched after them. So they were very afraid, and the children of Israel cried out to the LORD. Then they said to Moses, 'Because there were no graves in Egypt, have you taken us away to die in the wilderness? Why have you so dealt with us, to bring us up out of Egypt? Is this not the word that we told you in Egypt, saying, "Let us alone that we may serve the Egyptians?" For it would have been better for us to serve the Egyptians than that we should die in the wilderness.' And Moses said to the people, 'Do not be afraid. Stand still, and see the salvation of the LORD, which He will accomplish for you today. For the Egyptians whom you see today, you shall see again no more forever. The LORD will fight for you, and you shall hold your peace.'
. . . Then Moses stretched out his hand over the sea; and the LORD caused the sea to go back by a strong east wind all that night, and made the sea into dry land, and the waters

179

were divided. So the children of Israel went into the midst of the sea on the dry ground, and the waters were a wall to them on their right hand and on their left. And the Egyptians pursued and went after them into the midst of the sea, all Pharaoh's horses, his chariots, and his horsemen. Now it came to pass, in the morning watch, that the LORD looked down upon the army of the Egyptians through the pillar of fire and cloud, and He troubled the army of the Egyptians. And He took off the chariot wheels, so that they drove them with difficulty; and the Egyptians said, 'Let us flee from the face of Israel, for the LORD fights for them against the Egyptians.' . . . Then Miriam the prophetess, the sister of Aaron, took the timbrel in her hand; and all the women went out after her with timbrels and with dances. And Miriam answered them:

'Sing to the Lord,
For He has triumphed gloriously!
The horse and its rider
He has thrown into the sea!'" (14:10–14, 21–25; 15:20–21).

This is the word of the Lord.

Response: Thanks be to God.

Second Reader: A reading from Matthew: "Now after the Sabbath, as the first day of the week began to dawn, Mary Magdalene and the other Mary came to see the tomb. And behold, there was a great earthquake; for an angel of the Lord descended from heaven, and came and rolled back the stone from the door, and sat on it. His countenance was like lightning, and his clothing as white as snow. And the guards shook for fear of him, and became like dead men. But the angel answered and said to the women, 'Do not be afraid, for I know that you seek Jesus who was crucified. He is not here; for He is risen, as He said. Come, see the place where the Lord lay. And go quickly and tell His disciples that He is risen from the dead, and indeed He is going before you into Galilee; there you will see Him. Behold, I have told you.' So they departed quickly from the tomb with fear and great joy, and ran to bring His disciples word. And as they went to tell His disciples, behold, Jesus met them, saying, 'Rejoice!' And they came and held Him by the feet and worshiped Him. Then Jesus said to them, 'Do not be afraid. Go and tell My brethren to go to Galilee, and there they will see Me'" (28:1-10).

This is the word of the Lord.

Response: Thanks be to God.

We Respond to the Word of God

The Inquiry and Instruction

Question: I don't understand why we have a reading from Exodus on Easter Sunday.

Answer: The theme from Exodus and Matthew are the same.

Question: How so? One is about the Exodus, the other about the resurrection.

Answer: True. But the underlying theme of both is victory.

Question: Explain that.

Answer: In the Old Testament Pharaoh's power over Israel is a type of Satan's power over us. Moses led the people of Israel through the Red Sea and away from the Egyptians. This is their redemption, their freedom from bondage to Pharaoh. So, Christ's resurrection from the dead is His victory over Satan and the powers of evil which hold us bondage.

Question: So this is why Easter is the most important celebration of the Christian year?

Answer: Right. On this day we *especially* celebrate Christ's victory over evil and our reconciliation with the Father, the result of Christ's victory over death.

The Prayer of Response

(*Instruct everyone to repeat the response "His mercy endures forever" after each sentence or prayer.*)

Leader: Let us pray.

O give thanks to the Lord, for He is good!

Response: His mercy endures forever.

Leader: Let Israel now say,

Response: His mercy endures forever.

Leader: Let those who fear the Lord now say,

Response: His mercy endures forever.

Leader: Let the people in this home say,

Response: His mercy endures forever.

Leader: Lord, we will praise You. For You have an-swered our cry, and become our salvation. The stone the builders rejected has become the chief cornerstone. This was the Lord's doing; and it is marvelous in our eyes.

Response: His mercy endures forever.

Leader: O give thanks to the Lord, for He is good!

Response: His mercy endures forever.

(Adaptation of Ps. 118)

We Are Sent Forth

Leader: Receive the dismissal.
"If then you were raised with Christ, seek those things which are above, where Christ is, sitting at the right hand of God. Set your mind on things above, not on things on the earth. For you died, and your life is hidden with Christ in God. When Christ who is our life appears, then you also will appear with Him in glory" (Col. 3:1–4).

183

Response: Christ is risen! He is risen indeed!

All: Amen.

FIRST WEEK IN EASTER

We Prepare to Worship

Leader: Christ is risen!

Response: He is risen indeed!

Leader: The resurrection of Christ from the dead is an article of faith. We were not there when He rose from the grave, we did not stand before the empty tomb, we did not hear the angel say, "He is risen." We cannot, like Thomas, touch His wounded hands and feet, or feel the wound in His side. Yet we believe.

Let us pray.

Father, like Your servant Thomas, we desire proof and observation, and we struggle with uncertainty. Grant us the faith to believe. Open our eyes that we may see and our ears that we may hear. Fill our hearts with faith and give us lips of praise, that we may serve in joy the One who was raised from the dead to conquer sin in us and in the world. Through Jesus, our resurrected Lord, we pray. Amen.

Hymn: *Sing one of the following hymns:*
"Jesus Christ Is Risen Today"
"Up from the Grave He Arose"
"I Am the Resurrection and the Life"

We Listen to the Word of God

First   A reading from Genesis:

Reader: "Then God spoke to Noah and to his sons with him, saying: 'And as for Me, behold, I establish My covenant with you and with your descendants after you, and with every living creature that is with you: the birds, the cattle, and every beast of the earth with you, of all that go out of the ark, every beast of the earth. Thus I establish My covenant with you: Never again shall all flesh be cut off by the waters of the flood; never again shall there be a flood to destroy the earth.' And God said: 'This is the sign of the covenant which I make between Me and you, and every living creature that is with you, for perpetual generations: I set My rainbow in the cloud, and it shall be for the sign of the covenant between Me and the earth. It shall be, when I bring a cloud over the earth, that the rainbow shall be seen in the cloud; and I will remember My covenant which is between Me and you and every living creature of all flesh; the waters shall never again become a flood to destroy all flesh. The rainbow shall be in the cloud, and I will look on it to remember the everlasting covenant between God and every living creature of all flesh that is on the earth.' And God said to Noah. 'This is the sign of the covenant which I have established between Me and all flesh that is on the earth'" (9:8–17).

This is the word of the Lord.

Response: Thanks be to God.

Second Reader: "Then, the same day at evening, being the first day of the week, when the doors were shut where the disciples were assembled, for fear of the Jews, Jesus came and stood in the midst, and said to them, 'Peace be with you.' Now when He had said this, He showed them His hands and His side. Then the disciples were glad when they saw the Lord. Then Jesus said to them again, 'Peace to you! As the Father has sent Me, I also send you.' And when He had said this, He breathed on them, and said to them, 'Receive the Holy Spirit. If you forgive the sins of any, they are forgiven them; if you retain the sins of any, they are retained.' But Thomas, called Didymus, one of the twelve, was not with them when Jesus came. The other disciples therefore said to him, 'We have seen the Lord.' But he said to them, 'Unless I see in His hands the print of the nails, and put my finger into the print of the nails, and put my hand into His side, I will not believe.' And after eight days His disciples were again inside, and Thomas with them. Jesus came, the doors being shut, and stood in the midst, and said, 'Peace to you!' Then He said to Thomas, 'Reach your finger here, and look at My hands; and reach your hand here, and put it into My side. Do not be unbelieving, but believing.' And Thomas answered and said to Him, 'My Lord and my God!' Jesus said to him, 'Thomas, because you have seen Me, you have believed. Blessed are those who have not seen and yet have believed.' And truly Jesus did many other signs in the presence of His disciples, which are not written in this book; but these are written that you may believe that Jesus is the Christ, the Son of God, and that believing you may have life in His name" (John 20:19–31).

This is the word of the Lord.

Response: Thanks be to God.

We Respond to the Word of God

The Inquiry and Instruction

Question: What is the theme of this week's worship?

Answer: Doubting Thomas is the focus of our gospel reading. But the real theme is faith that does not demand proof.

Question: Why did Thomas demand proof of the resurrection?

Answer: It is simply a human desire to want proof in order to believe.

Question: What does Jesus teach us in this incident?

Answer: He doesn't put down the human desire for proof, but He does emphasize the glory of believing even in the absence of proof.

Question: Do we have proof of the resurrection today?

Answer: Not the kind that Thomas demanded.

Question: Is there another kind?

Answer: We have the witness of Scripture to the resurrection of Jesus. John wrote, "These are written that you may believe that Jesus is the Christ, the Son of God, and that believing you may have life in His name" (20:31).

The Prayer of Response

Leader: Let us pray.

Lord, I will praise You with my whole heart.
Your works are great;
They are honorable and glorious,
And Your righteousness endures forever.
You are gracious and full of compassion.
What You do is done in truth and
    uprightness.
You have sent redemption to Your people;
You have commanded a covenant forever.
Holy and awesome is Your name. Amen.
(Adaptation of Ps. 111)

We Are Sent Forth

Leader: Receive the dismissal.
"Blessed be the God and Father of our Lord
Jesus Christ, who according to His abundant

mercy has begotten us again to a living hope through the resurrection of Jesus from the dead" (1 Pet. 1:3).

Response: Christ is risen! He is risen indeed!

SECOND WEEK IN EASTER

We Prepare to Worship

Leader: Christ is risen!

Response: He is risen indeed!

Leader: My dear family, as Christian people our earnest desire is to know the Lord. There are many ways He can be known. He is known through His word, He is known through preaching, He is known in prayer and even in song. This week we contemplate how He is known in the breaking of the bread.

Let us pray.

Lord Jesus, on the night when You were betrayed You took bread, broke it, and said "This is My body." Likewise You took the cup of wine and said, "This is My blood of the New Covenant." Help us, like the disciples on the road to Emmaus, to discern Your presence in the symbols of bread and wine when we celebrate Your remembrance. Through Jesus Christ our Lord. Amen.

Hymn: *Sing one of the following hymns:*
          "He Is Risen, He Is Risen!"
          "Christ the Lord Is Risen Today"
          "He Is Here"

We Listen to the Word of God

First   A reading from Acts:
Reader: "But Peter, standing up with the eleven, raised
          his voice and said to them, . . . 'Therefore let
          all the house of Israel know assuredly that
          God has made this Jesus, whom you crucified,
          both Lord and Christ.' Now when they heard
          this, they were cut to the heart, and said to
          Peter and the rest of the apostles, 'Men and
          brethren, what shall we do?' Then Peter said
          to them, 'Repent, and let every one of you be
          baptized in the name of Jesus Christ for the
          remission of sins; and you shall receive the gift
          of the Holy Spirit. For the promise is to you
          and to your children, and to all who are afar
          off, as many as the Lord our God will call.'
          And with many other words he testified and
          exhorted them, saying, 'Be saved from this
          perverse generation'" (2:14, 36–40).

          This is the word of the Lord.

Response: Thanks be to God.

Second   A reading from the gospel of Luke:
Reader: "Now behold, two of them were traveling that
          same day to a village called Emmaus, which
          was about seven miles from Jerusalem. And
          they talked together of all these things which

had happened. So it was, while they con-
versed and reasoned, that Jesus Himself drew
near and went with them. But their eyes were
restrained, so that they did not know
Him. . . . Then they drew near to the village
where they were going, and He indicated that
He would have gone farther. But they con-
strained him, saying, 'Abide with us, for it is
toward evening, and the day is far spent.' And
He went in to stay with them. Now it came to
pass, as He sat at the table with them, that He
took bread, blessed and broke it, and gave it
to them. Then their eyes were opened and
they knew Him; and He vanished from their
sight. And they said to one another, 'Did not
our heart burn within us while He talked with
us on the road, and while He opened the
Scriptures to us?' So they rose up that very
hour and returned to Jerusalem, and found
the eleven and those who were with them
gathered together, saying, 'The Lord is risen
indeed, and has appeared to Simon!' And
they told about the things that had happened
on the road, and how He was known to them
in the breaking of bread" (24:13–16, 28–35).

This is the word of the Lord.

Response: Thanks be to God.

We Respond to the Word of God
The Inquiry and Instruction
Question: What is the point of the story about the disciples on the road to Damascus?

Answer: It is really the same as that from our reading in Acts.

Question: Which is what?

Answer: Look closely at Peter's sermon, and you will see the point in these words, "God has made this Jesus, whom you crucified, both Lord and Christ" (Acts 2:36).

Question: You mean that the disciples are to hear and believe the message that Jesus is the Messiah?

Answer: Yes.

Question: But I don't see that in Luke's account.

Answer: Look at it more closely.

Question: How?

Answer: The disciples did not know Jesus to be the Messiah.

Question: Until He broke bread?

Answer: Right.

Question: What does that mean for us today?

Answer: It means that today when we take communion we are to discern the risen Christ who is the Messiah, our Lord.

The Prayer of Response

Leader: Let us pray.

Lord, as wheat is harvested from the fields and brought into a single loaf; so may we who are members of Your church universal be gathered together at Your table through Jesus Christ, our Lord. Amen.

We Are Sent Forth

Leader: Receive the dismissal.

"You were not redeemed with corruptible things, like silver or gold, from your aimless conduct received by tradition from your fathers, but with the precious blood of Christ, as of a lamb without blemish and without spot" (1 Pet. 1:18–19).

Response: Christ is risen! He is risen indeed.

THIRD WEEK IN EASTER

We Prepare to Worship

Leader: Christ is risen!

Response: He is risen indeed!

Leader: Dear people of God, our Lord Jesus, who died for us and was raised for our salvation, frequently used illustrations from contemporary life to teach truth. Today, we recall one of those images, namely, the image of sheep and the shepherd. We are His sheep and He is our Shepherd.

Let us pray.

Lord Jesus, You who have been raised from the dead to shepherd Your flock, we, Your sheep, call upon You, O Shepherd, to lead and guide us in the way of truth and righteousness for Your sake. Amen.

Hymn: *Sing one of the following hymns:*
"At the Lamb's High Feast We Sing"
"He Lives"
"O the Wonder of It All"

We Listen to the Word of God

First Reader: A reading from Acts:

"And after the reading of the Law and the Prophets, the rulers of the synagogue sent to them saying, 'Men and brethren, if you have any word of exhortation for the people, say on.' Then Paul stood up, and motioning with his hand said, 'Men of Israel, and you who fear God, listen: . . . Men and brethren, sons of the family of Abraham, and those among you who fear God, to you the word of this salvation has been sent. For those who dwell in Jerusalem, and for their rulers, because they did not know Him, nor even the voices of the Prophets which are read every Sabbath, have fulfilled them in condemning Him. And though they found no cause for death in Him, they asked Pilate that He should be put to death. Now when they had fulfilled all that was written concerning Him, they took Him down from the tree and laid Him in a tomb. But God raised Him from the dead. He was seen for many days by those who came up with Him from Galilee to Jerusalem, who are His witnesses to the people. And we declare to you glad tidings—that promise which was made to the fathers. God has fulfilled this for us their children, in that He has raised up Jesus. As it is also written in the second Psalm: "You are My Son, / Today I have begotten You"'" (13:15–16, 26–33).

This is the word of the Lord.

Response: Thanks be to God.

Second Reader: A reading from the gospel according to John: "'Most assuredly, I say to you, he who does not enter the sheepfold by the door, but climbs up some other way, the same is a thief and a robber. But he who enters by the door is the shepherd of the sheep. To him the doorkeeper opens, and the sheep hear his voice; and he calls his own sheep by name and leads them out. And when he brings out his own sheep, he goes on before them; and the sheep follow him, for they know his voice. Yet they will by no means follow a stranger, but will flee from him, for they do not know the voice of strangers.' Jesus used this illustration, but they did not understand the things which He spoke to them. Then Jesus said to them again, 'Most assuredly, I say to you, I am the door of the sheep. All who ever came before Me are thieves and robbers, but the sheep did not hear them. I am the door. If anyone enters by Me, he will be saved, and will go in and out and find pasture. The thief does not come except to steal, and to kill, and to destroy. I have come that they may have life, and that they may have it more abundantly.' . . . Now it was the Feast of Dedication in Jerusalem, and it was winter. And Jesus walked in the temple, in Solomon's porch. Then the Jews surrounded Him and said to Him, 'How long do you keep us in doubt? If You are the Christ, tell us plainly.' Jesus answered them, 'I told you, and you do not believe. The works that I do in My Father's name, they bear witness of Me. But you do not believe, because you are not of My sheep, as I said to you. My sheep hear My voice, and I know them, and they follow Me. And I give them eternal life, and they shall never perish; neither shall anyone snatch them out of My hand. My Father, who has given them to Me, is greater than all; and no one is able to snatch them out of My Father's hand. I and My Father are one'" (10:1–10, 22–30).

This is the word of the Lord.

Response: Thanks be to God.

We Respond to the Word of God

The Inquiry and Instruction

Question: I am going to tell you some characteristics of sheep, and you are going to tell me the implication of this characteristic for us as God's sheep. First, sheep are timid and defenseless.

Answer: As Christians we should not pick fights and be critical of each other.

Question: Sheep follow their leader.

Answer: Our leader is Jesus, and we are to do His will.

Question: Sheep flock together.

Answer: The church is Christ's flock. We should not stray from the people of God.

Question: Now, I am going to tell you some characteristics of a shepherd, and you will respond with its meaning for us as Christians. First, a shepherd cares for his flock of sheep.

Answer: The writer of Hebrews describes Jesus as "that great Shepherd of the sheep" (13:20). This means that He loves us dearly and cares about every aspect of our lives.

Question: A shepherd protects his flock and seeks out those who are lost.

Answer: Peter refers to some Christians as "sheep going astray, [who] have now returned to the Shepherd and Overseer of your souls" (1 Pet. 2:25). Christ our Shepherd cares about our eternal destiny. When we stray from Him, He calls for us and seeks us out.

The Prayer of Response

Leader: Let us pray.

Lord, You are our shepherd;
We shall not want.
You make us to lie down in green pastures;
You lead us beside the still waters,
You restore our soul;
You lead us in the paths of righteousness
For your name's sake.
Yea, though we walk through the valley of the
shadow of death,
We will fear no evil;
For you are with us;
Your rod and your staff, they comfort us.
You prepare a table before us in the presence
of our enemies;
You anoint our head with oil;
Our cup runs over.
Surely goodness and mercy shall follow us
all the days of our lives;
And we will dwell in the house of the Lord
forever. Amen.

(Adaptation of Ps. 23)

We Are Sent Forth

Leader: Receive the dismissal:
"After these things I looked, and behold, a
great multitude which no one could number,
of all nations, tribes, peoples, and tongues,
standing before the throne and before the
Lamb, clothed with white robes, with palm

branches in their hands, and crying out with a loud voice, saying, 'Salvation belongs to our God who sits on the throne, and to the Lamb!' And all the angels stood around the throne and the elders and the four living creatures, and fell on their faces before the throne and worshiped God, saying:
'Amen! Blessing and glory and wisdom,
Thanksgiving and honor and power and might
Be to our God forever and ever. Amen'"
(Rev. 7:9–12).

Response: Christ is risen! He is risen indeed!

FOURTH WEEK IN EASTER

We Prepare to Worship

Leader: Christ is risen!

Response: He is risen indeed!

Leader: After the resurrection our Lord alone knew that He would ascend into heaven. It was His plan from the beginning to send the Holy Spirit and form the little band of disciples into the church. This week we recall His words of preparation spoken to the disciples.

Let us pray.

Lord Jesus Christ, we bless You for the plans You make for us, for You have not left us, nor have You forsaken us. You now prepare for us a dwelling place; for in Your Father's house are many mansions, and where You are we shall someday be. Grant us, O Lord, peace of mind and courage to live in the expectancy of Your return, and in the certainty of our eternal home, through Jesus Christ our Lord. Amen.

Hymn: *Sing one of the following hymns:*
"Come Ye Faithful, Raise the Strain"
"I Know That My Redeemer Liveth"
"God Is So Good"

We Listen to the Word of God

**First
Reader:** A reading from the first epistle of Peter:
"Therefore, laying aside all malice, all guile, hypocrisy, envy, and all evil speaking, as new-born babes, desire the pure milk of the word, that you may grow thereby, if indeed you have tasted that the Lord is gracious. Coming to Him as a living stone, rejected indeed by men, but chosen by God and precious, you also, as living stones, are being built up a spiritual house, a holy priesthood, to offer up spiritual sacrifices acceptable to God through Jesus Christ" (2:1–5).

This is the word of the Lord.

Response: Thanks be to God.

**Second
Reader:** A reading from the gospel according to John:
"'Let not your heart be troubled; you believe

in God, believe also in Me. In My Father's house are many mansions, if it were not so, I would have told you. I go to prepare a place for you. And if I go and prepare a place for you, I will come again and receive you to Myself; that where I am, there you may be also. And where I go you know, and the way you know.' Thomas said to Him, 'Lord, we do not know where You are going, and how can we know the way?' Jesus said to him, 'I am the way, the truth, and the life. No one comes to the Father except through Me. If you had known Me, you would have known My Father also; and from now on you know Him and have seen Him.' Philip said to Him, 'Lord, show us the Father, and it is sufficient for us.' Jesus said to him, 'Have I been with you so long, and yet you have not known Me, Philip? He who has seen Me has seen the Father, so how can you say, "Show us the Father?" Do you not believe that I am in the Father, and the Father in Me? The words that I speak to you I do not speak on My own authority; but the Father who dwells in Me does the works. Believe Me that I am in the Father and the Father in Me, or else believe Me for the sake of the works themselves. Most assuredly, I say to you, he who believes in Me, the works that I do he will do also; and greater works than these he will do, because I go to My Father. And whatever you ask in My name, that I will do, that the Father may be glorified in the

Son. If you ask anything in My name, I will
do it'" (14:1–14).

This is the word of the Lord.

Response: Thanks be to God.

We Respond to the Word of God

The Inquiry and Instruction

Question: In the opening statement we said this week's
emphasis was on the preparation of the disciples for their life without the presence of
Christ after the Ascension. How does this
connect with the reading from 1 Peter?

Answer: The church, which is Christ's body, is the
means by which Jesus remains in contact with
His disciples. Christ is, as our gospel says,
"the way, the truth, and the life."

Question: Has Christ entrusted His gospel to the
church?

Answer: Yes. Christ has appointed the church to be
the visible manifestation of Himself in the
world. The church preaches Christ and so
shows us the way to the Father.

Question: Is the church like the continuing presence of
Christ in the world?

Answer: Right, it is the body of Christ, His special
people who proclaim His praises.

The Prayer of Response

Leader: Let us pray.

O Lord our God,
You who brought the Church into being
And called us into the body of Your Son,
We make a joyful shout to You;
We sing out the honor of Your name;
We make glorious Your praise.
How awesome are Your works!
Through the greatness of Your power,
Your enemies shall submit to You.
All the earth shall worship You and sing
    praises to You;
They shall sing praises
To Your name. Amen.

(Adaptation of Ps. 66:1–14)

We Are Sent Forth

Leader: Receive the dismissal:
"Let not your heart be troubled. You believe
in God, believe also in me," for "you are a
chosen generation, a royal priesthood, a holy
nation . . . who once were not a people, but
now are the people of God" (John 14:1;
1 Pet. 2:9–10).

Christ is risen!

Response: He is risen indeed!

FIFTH WEEK IN EASTER

We Prepare to Worship

Leader: Christ is risen!

Response: He is risen indeed!

Leader: We are drawing near to the close of the Easter season. During this time we see our Lord preparing His disciples for what lies ahead. He knows that they may feel forsaken after His ascension. But, as our Lord did not forsake Israel, so he will not forsake His disciples. He will send them the Holy Spirit.

Let us pray.

Lord God, You did not forsake Israel, nor has Your Son Jesus Christ forsaken us. We bless you for sending Your Holy Spirit to dwell within us, to bring us the presence of Jesus, and to illumine our paths. Lead us, O Lord, by Your Spirit into the truth of Your Son and into a relationship with Him who, with the Holy Spirit, abides in union with You forevermore. Amen.

Hymn: *Sing one of the following hymns:*
"Jesus Lives!"
"Come Ye Faithful, Raise the Strain"
"We Are One in the Spirit"

We Listen to the Word of God

First Reader: A reading from Isaiah:

"When the poor and needy seek water, and
there is none,
And their tongues fail for thirst,
I, the LORD, will hear them;
I, the God of Israel, will not forsake
them. . . .
I will make the wilderness a pool of water,
And the dry land springs of water.
I will plant in the wilderness the cedar and
the acacia tree,
The myrtle and the oil tree;
I will set in the desert the cypress tree and the
pine
And the box tree together,
That they may see and know,
And consider and understand together,
That the hand of the LORD has done this,
And the Holy One of Israel has created it"
(41:17–20).

Reader: This is the word of the Lord.

Response: Thanks be to God.

Second Reader: A reading from the gospel according to John:

"If you love Me, keep My commandments.
And I will pray the Father, and He will give
you another Helper, that He may abide with
you forever, even the Spirit of truth, whom
the world cannot receive, because it neither
sees Him nor knows Him; but you know Him,
for He dwells with you and will be in you. I

will not leave you orphans; I will come to you. A little while longer and the world will see Me no more, but you will see Me. Because I live, you will live also. At that day you will know that I am in My Father, and you in Me, and I in you. He who has My commandments and keeps them, it is he who loves Me. And he who loves Me will be loved by My Father, and I will love him and manifest Myself to him" (14:15–21).

This is the word of the Lord.

Response: Thanks be to God.

We Respond to the Word of God

The Inquiry and Instruction

Question: What is the emphasis of our worship this week?

Answer: The coming of the Holy Spirit.

Question: Why did God send the Holy Spirit?

Answer: Christ ascended into the heavens. But through the Holy Spirit He continues to be present with us in the church.

Question: What does the Holy Spirit do?

Answer: The Holy Spirit is present in our worship. He brings the power and presence of Christ to us through preaching and the celebration of communion.

Question: What does the Holy Spirit do as He lives within us?

Answer: The Bible speaks about our bearing the fruits of the Holy Spirit. "The fruit of the Spirit is love, joy, peace, longsuffering, kindness, goodness, faithfulness, gentleness, self-control" (Gal. 5:22–23).

The Prayer of Response

Leader: Let us pray.

Lord, You who have given us
Your Holy Spirit,
Your praise comes from the heavens;
The heights praise You;
The angels praise You;
All the heavenly hosts praise You;
Sun and Moon praise You;
All the stars of light praise You;
The heaven of heavens and the water above
    the heavens praise You!
Fire and hail, snow and clouds praise You;
Stormy winds, mountains and hills,
Fruitful trees and all cedars praise You!
Bees and all cattle;
Creeping things and flying fowl praise You!
Kings of the earth and all peoples;
Princes and all judges of the earth praise You!
Young men and children praise You!
Old men and children praise You!
Lord, Your name alone is exalted;
Your glory is above the earth and heaven;
This we join with creation
And all the saints to cry. Amen.

(Adaptation of Ps. 148)

We Are Sent Forth

Leader: Receive the dismissal.
"I am the vine, you are the branches. He who abides in me, and I in him, bears much fruit" (John 15:5).

Leader: Christ is risen!

Response: He is risen indeed!

SIXTH WEEK IN EASTER: ASCENSION DAY

We Prepare to Worship

Leader: Christ is risen!

Response: He is risen indeed!

Leader: My dear family, on this day long ago our Lord, who was raised from the dead, ascended into heaven and was seated at the right hand of the Father. There He will remain until all His enemies have been put under His feet, then He will come again to receive us to Himself and to establish the new heavens and the new earth.

Let us pray.

Lord Jesus, You who came from heaven to live among us, to die for us, and to be raised again for our salvation, You, the ascended Lord, we worship and adore. We hymn Your praises and sing of Your glory, and we await Your coming again to receive us to Yourself. "Even so, come, Lord Jesus!" (Rev. 22:20) Amen.

Hymn: *Sing one of the following hymns:*
"Look Ye Saints"
"My Faith Looks Up to Thee"
"We're Going to Lift Up the Name of Jesus"

We Listen to the Word of God

First Reader: A reading from Acts:
"The former account I made, O Theophilus, of all that Jesus began both to do and teach, until the day in which He was taken up, after He through the Holy Spirit had given commandments to the apostles whom He had chosen, to whom He also presented Himself alive after His suffering by many infallible proofs, being seen by them during forty days and speaking of the things pertaining to the kingdom of God. And being assembled together with them, He commanded them not to depart from Jerusalem, but to wait for the Promise of the Father, 'which,' He said, 'you have heard from Me; for John truly baptized with water, but you shall be baptized with the Holy Spirit not many days from now.' Therefore, when they had come together, they asked Him, saying, 'Lord, will You at this time restore the kingdom to Israel?' And He said to them, 'It is not for you to know times or sea-

sons which the Father has put in His own authority. But you shall receive power when the Holy Spirit has come upon you; and you shall be witnesses to Me in Jerusalem, and in all Judea and Samaria, and to the end of the earth.' Now when He had spoken these things, while they watched, He was taken up, and a cloud received Him out of their sight. And while they looked steadfastly toward heaven as He went up, behold, two men stood by them in white apparel, who also said, 'Men of Galilee, why do you stand gazing up into heaven?'" (1:1–11).

This is the word of the Lord.

Response: Thanks be to God.

Second Reader: A reading from the gospel according to Mark: "Now when He rose early on the first day of the week, He appeared first to Mary Magdalene, out of whom He had cast seven demons. She went and told those who had been with Him, as they mourned and wept. And when they heard that He was alive and had been seen by her, they did not believe. After that, He appeared in another form to two of them as they walked and went into the country. And they went and told it to the rest, but they did not believe them either. Afterward He appeared to the eleven as they sat at the table; and He rebuked their unbelief and hardness of heart, because they did not believe those who had seen Him after He had risen. And He said to them, 'Go into all the world and preach the gospel to every creature.' . . . So then, after the Lord had spoken to them, He was received up into heaven, and sat down at the right hand of God. And they went out and preached everywhere, the Lord working with them and confirming the word through the accompanying signs. Amen" (16:9–15, 19–20).

This is the word of the Lord.

Response: Thanks be to God.

We Respond to the Word of God

The Inquiry and Instruction

Question: What do we focus on this week?

Answer: The focus of our Scripture readings is the Ascension. However, the text contains a summary of the events in Jesus' life from His resurrection to the Ascension. In these times He prepared His people to become the church.

Question: What else?

Answer: The text also points our hearts into the future, into the expectancy of Christ's return.

Question: What is the meaning of the Ascension for us today?

Answer: It calls attention to the task of evangelism that God's people are to assume. We need to

211

focus on the Great Commission: "Go into all the world and preach the gospel to every creature" (Mark 16:15).

The Prayer of Response

Leader: Let us pray.

Lord God, Your Son Jesus has gone up with a shout,
With the sound of the trumpet.
We sing praises to You, O God,
For Your Son is our King.
Your Son is King of all the earth.
He reigns over the nations;
He sits upon His Holy Throne;
He is greatly exalted.

(Adaptation of Ps. 47:5–9)

All: Amen.

We Are Sent Forth

Leader: Receive the dismissal.
"Go therefore and make disciples of all the nations, baptizing them in the name of the Father and of the Son and of the Holy Spirit, teaching them to observe all things that I have commanded you; and lo, I am with you always, even to the end of the age. Amen" (Matt. 28:19–20).

Christ is risen!

Response: He is risen indeed!

SEVENTH WEEK IN EASTER

We Prepare to Worship

Leader: Christ is risen!

Response: He is risen indeed!

Leader: Our Lord Jesus Christ—whose birth, life, death, resurrection, and ascension we have celebrated since Advent—is now seated at the right hand of the Father. He has been received up into the heavens where He has been glorified. And we who have been left behind, whose task it is to proclaim Christ and to live by His name, are also called to give Him great glory.

Let us pray.

Lord Jesus Christ, we proclaim Your glory; for You gave up the glory that You had with the Father before the world began, to become one of us, to live in our world, to participate in our life, to endure our suffering, even to death. Now, with the Father and the Holy Spirit, You are glorified, one God forever and ever. Amen.

Hymn: *Sing one of the following hymns:*
"The Head That Once Was Crowned with Thorns"
"Praise to the Lord"
"Alleluia"

We Listen to the Word of God

First   A reading from Revelation:
Reader: " 'And behold, I am coming quickly, and My reward is with Me, to give to everyone according to his work. I am the Alpha and the Omega, the Beginning and the End, the First and the Last.' Blessed are those who do His commandments, that they may have the right to the tree of life, and may enter through the gates into the city. . . . 'I, Jesus, have sent My angel to testify to you these things in the churches. I am the Root and the Offspring of David, the Bright and Morning Star.' And the Spirit and the bride say, 'Come!' and let him who hears say, 'Come!' And let him who thirsts come. And whoever desires, let him take the water of life freely. He who testifies to these things says, 'Surely I am coming quickly.' Amen. Even so, come, Lord Jesus!" (22:12–14, 16–17, 20).

This is the word of the Lord.

Response: Thanks be to God.

Second   A reading from the gospel according to John:
Reader: "I do not pray for these alone, but also for those who will believe in Me through their word; that they all may be one, as You, Father, are in Me, and I in You; that they also may be one in Us, that the world may believe that You sent Me. And the glory which You gave Me I have given them, that they may be one just as We are one: I in them, and You in Me;

that they may be made perfect in one, and that the world may know that You have sent Me, and have loved them as You have loved Me. Father, I desire that they also whom You gave Me may be with Me where I am, that they may behold My glory which You have given Me; for You loved Me before the foundation of the world. O righteous Father! The world has not known You; but I have known You; and these have known that You sent Me. And I have declared to them Your name, and will declare it, that the love with which You loved Me may be in them, and I in them" (17:20–26).

This is the word of the Lord.

Response: Thanks be to God.

We Respond to the Word of God

The Inquiry and Instruction

Question: What is the main point of today's gospel reading?

Answer: The glory of Christ.

Question: What does it mean to say that Christ is *glorified*?

Answer: For us the word means "respect" or "renown." In the Hebrew culture at the time of Christ the word meant "a value that elicits respect."

Question: Can you give an example?

Answer: Yes. God's glory is manifested in His actions. For example, God received great glory for bringing the people of Israel across the Red Sea.

Question: Is there a New Testament example?

Answer: Yes. The example in our text is excellent. Christ refers to the glory He had with the Father before the creation of the world. The text indicates that Christ has glorified the Father by carrying out His task of redemption. Now, the Father glorifies the Son.

Question: In what other ways has the Son given glory to the Father?

Answer: He has made the Father known to us.

Question: And how is Jesus glorified?

Answer: In His disciples. In us. As we do Christ's will, Christ is glorified even as the Father is glorified when the Son does His will.

The Prayer of Response

Lord, we clap our hands and shout to You
With the voice of triumph;
For You, the Lord Most High, are awesome.
You are a great King over all the earth.
You will subdue all the people and all the
    nations.
Great and Holy is Your name;
Your glory is unspeakable
And Your name is everlasting. Amen.
(Adaptation of Ps. 47:1–4)

We Are Sent Forth

Leader: Receive the dismissal.
Bring glory to the Father and to the Son and to the Holy Spirit. As it was in the beginning, let it be now and forever.

Christ is risen!

Response: He is risen indeed!

PENTECOST SUNDAY

We Prepare to Worship

Leader: Today is a very special day in the life of the church. On this day long ago, the Holy Spirit came upon the church in great power and might. Today we celebrate that great event. We ought therefore to be mindful of the presence and power of the Holy Spirit in our lives and in that of the church.

Hymn: *Sing one of the following hymns:*
"O Come, Creator Spirit, Come"
"Breathe on Me, Breath of God"
"Holy Spirit, Come"

We Listen to the Word of God

First Reader: A reading from Joel:
"And it shall come to pass afterward
That I will pour out My Spirit on all flesh;

Your sons and your daughters shall prophesy,
Your old men shall dream dreams,
Your young men shall see visions;
And also on My menservants and on My
    maidservants
I will pour out My Spirit in those days.
And I will show wonders in the heavens and
    in the earth:
Blood and fire and pillars of smoke.
The sun shall be turned into darkness,
And the moon into blood,
Before the coming of the great and terrible
    day of the LORD.
And it shall come to pass
That whoever calls on the name of the LORD
    shall be saved.
For in Mount Zion and in Jerusalem there
    shall be deliverance,
As the LORD has said,
Among the remnant whom the LORD calls
(2:28–32).

This is the word of the Lord.

Response: Thanks be to God.

Second   A reading from Acts:
Reader: "Now when the Day of Pentecost had fully
come, they were all with one accord in one
place. And suddenly there came a sound from
heaven, as of a rushing mighty wind, and it
filled the whole house where they were sitting. Then there appeared to them divided
tongues, as of fire, and one sat upon each of

them. And they were all filled with the Holy Spirit and began to speak with other tongues, as the Spirit gave them utterance. Now there were dwelling in Jerusalem Jews, devout men, from every nation under heaven. And when this sound occurred, the multitude came together, and were confused, because everyone heard them speak in his own language. Then they were all amazed and marveled, saying to one another, 'Look, are not all these who speak Galileans? And how is it that we hear, each in our own language in which we were born? Parthians and Medes and Elamites, those dwelling in Mesopotamia, Judea and Cappadocia, Pontus and Asia, Phyrgia and Pamphylia, Egypt and the parts of Libya adjoining Cyrene, visitors from Rome, both Jews and proselytes, Cretans and Arabs—we hear them speaking in our own tongues the wonderful works of God'" (2:1–11).

This is the word of the Lord.

Response: Thanks be to God.

We Respond to the Word of God

The Inquiry and Instruction

Question: What does the word *Pentecost* mean?

Answer: It simply means "fifty." In Jewish times the Feast of Weeks was celebrated fifty days after Passover. Fifty days after the resurrection, the Holy Spirit came.

Question: What do we celebrate on Pentecost?

Answer: Three things. First, the coming of the Holy Spirit. Both the reading from Joel and the gospel prefigure the coming of the Holy Spirit to reside in the Christian, and in the church.

Question: And the second?

Answer: The beginning of the church. Pentecost, you might say, is the birthday celebration of the church.

Question: You said there are three things we celebrate.

Answer: Yes, we also recall the words of Jesus, "As the Father has sent me, I also send you" (John 20:21).

The Prayer of Response

Leader: Let us pray.

Lord, we believe Your eye is upon those who
    fear You,
Those who have hope in You.
Lord, we wait upon You;
For You are our help and our shield.
Our hearts rejoice in You
Because we have trusted in Your holy name.
Lord, let Your mercy be upon us
As we hope in You,
And send upon us
Your Holy Spirit, we pray. Amen.
(Adaptation of Ps. 33:18–22)

We Are Sent Forth

Leader: Receive the dismissal.

"But you shall receive power when the Holy Spirit has come upon you; and you shall be witnesses to Me in Jerusalem, and in all Judea and Samaria, and to the end of the earth" (Acts 1:8).

Response: Thanks be to God.

PART II

Family Reading for the Nonfestive Time of the Year

PENTECOST

PENTECOST The cross and triangle have long been the means of expressing the mystic nature of the triune Godhead and Christ's
essence. The addition of the Paraclete (above) suggests to
worshipers the coming of the Holy Spirit from above.

INTRODUCTION TO
the Nonfestive Season

Traditionally the church year follows the life of Christ for the first half of the year (Advent to Pentecost) and then, during the second half of the year, it follows the life of the early church through the first century.

There are advantages to following the life of Christ for half a year and the early church for the other half of the year in family devotions. The first half of the year is more worship-centered and the last half more instructional. This twofold emphasis brings the family into contact with the two traditions of an experienced Christianity and an intellectual Christianity.

During the gospel side of the church year the intent for family devotions is to allow the sequence of Advent, Christmas, Epiphany, Lent, Holy Week, Easter, and Pentecost to order our inner experience of Christ. This sequence brings us through the events in Christ's life that organize our spiritual pilgrimage along the lines of repentance, faith, conversion, and new life in Christ. By going through this cycle on a yearly basis our hearts and lives are continually renewed and refreshed.

However, in addition to the gospels, the New Testament contains the book of Acts and the Epistles. These books continue the story of Christ through the story of the early church. The church is the great response to Christ. It is the context in which Christ continues to be present in and to the world. Since we are not only of Christ but of the church, it is fitting that we recall the formative days of the church in the apostolic era. The following devotions are designed to lead you from the church's inception to the close of the apostolic age.

For the sake of convenience I have organized our study into six monthly periods. In each monthly study I have emphasized a step in the progress and development of the church. Since the dominant figure of the New Testament church is Paul, I have organized much of the history of the developing church around his activities. This method of organization is not unusual since it is simply borrowed from Luke, the author of Acts.

However, one additional feature will allow the family study to proceed as a story. The feature of which I speak is the organization of the New Testament epistles into the historical sequence in which they were written, inserting them in the appropriate historical narrative of Acts. Frequently the New Testament books are studied out of context. Since most of the books were written to meet a specific critical need in the church of the first century, violence is done to the nature and meaning of the book when it is read apart from its natural context.

In each study I have accented the special theme dealt with by the narrative or the epistle. Whenever possible I have indicated where in Acts mention may be found regarding the historical setting of the book. Then, in a theme verse, I have isolated a short passage for discussion or memorization so that the theme will stand out even more. The Scripture reading expands on the theme, and the study is closed with prayer.

June: The Primitive Church A.D. 30–49

FIRST WEEK: THE EARLY CHURCH

Theme: Apostolic Authority

The mark of the earliest community of Christian churches is the centrality of the apostles. Those who had been with Christ during His three-year ministry were immediately recognized as the authoritative interpreters of His life, death, and resurrection. Luke, the author of the Acts of the Apostles, takes great pains to develop a picture of the central role of the apostles in worship and in preaching. In particular, the sermons of the apostles provide us with the earliest interpretation of Jesus.

Background: The events of Acts 1–7.

Theme Verse: Acts 2:42: "They continued steadfastly in the apostles' doctrine and fellowship, in the breaking of bread, and in prayers."

Reading: Acts 3:11–21. Peter's sermon at Solomon's Portico.

"Now as the lame man who was healed held on to Peter and John, all the people ran together to them in the porch which is called Solomon's, greatly amazed. So when Peter saw it, he responded to the people: 'Men of Israel, why do you marvel at this? Or why look so intently at us, as though by our own power or godliness we had made this man walk? The God of Abraham, Isaac, and Jacob, the God of our fathers, glorified His Servant Jesus, whom you delivered up and denied in the presence of Pilate, when he was determined to let Him go. But you denied the Holy One and the Just, and asked for a murderer to be granted to you, and killed the Prince of life, whom God raised from the dead, of which we are witnesses. And His name, through faith in His name, has made this man strong, whom you see and know. Yes, the faith which comes through Him has given him this perfect soundness in the presence of you all. Yet now, brethren, I know that you did it in ignorance, as did also your rulers. But those things which God foretold by the mouth of all His prophets, that the Christ would suffer, He has thus fulfilled. Repent therefore and be converted, that your sins may be blotted out, so that times of refreshing may come from the presence of the Lord, and that He may send Jesus Christ, who was preached to you before, whom heaven must receive until the time of restoration of all things, which God has spoken by the mouth of all His holy prophets since the world began.'"

Prayer: Father in heaven, we bless You for Peter Your apostle, who by his preaching and example left us a witness to the death and resurrection of Your Son. May we, like him, call sinners into repentance and conversion. Through Jesus Christ, our Lord, we pray. Amen.

June: The Primitive Church A.D. 30–49

SECOND WEEK:
THE CONVERSION OF SAUL

Theme: God Chooses the Unlikely

The young Christian community soon fell under severe persecution for preaching Christ as Messiah and Lord. The best known persecutor of the church was a young man named Saul, who "made havoc of the church, entering every house, and dragging off men and women, committing them to prison" (Acts 8:3). Yet, it was this person whom God chose to be the greatest missionary and teacher of the first century. In choosing Saul, God was preparing through him to reach out beyond Israel into the Gentile community.

Background: The events of Acts 8–9.

Theme Verse: Acts 9:15: "He is a chosen vessel of Mine to bear My name before the Gentiles, kings, and the children of Israel."

Reading: Acts 9:20–27. Saul preaches Christ.

"Immediately he preached the Christ in the synagogues, that He is the Son of God. Then all who heard were amazed, and said, 'Is this not he who destroyed those who called on this name in Jerusalem, and has come here for that purpose, so that he might bring them bound to the chief priests?' But Saul increased all the more in strength, and confounded the Jews who dwelt in Damascus, proving that this Jesus is the Christ. Now after many days were past, the Jews plotted to kill him. But their plot became known to Saul. And they watched the gates day and night, to kill him. Then the disciples took him by night and let him down through the wall in a large basket. And when Saul had come to Jerusalem, he tried to join the disciples; but they were all afraid of him, and did not believe that he was a disciple. But Barnabas took him and brought him to the apostles. And he declared to them how he had seen the Lord on the road, and that He had spoken to him, and how he had preached boldly at Damascus in the name of Jesus."

Prayer: Lord, as Paul responded to Your call, committed his life to You, and declared You to be the Son of God, so may we, who have been called by You, believe in You and spread Your good news to others. Through Jesus Christ our Lord we pray. Amen.

June: The Primitive Church: A.D. 30–49

THIRD WEEK: THE MISSION EXPANDS

Theme: The Gentiles Are Included as God's People

The first Christians were Jews, and they believed that Jesus' death and resurrection was for them alone. But God's plan was much more expansive than their limited imaginations would allow. The death of His Son was for the whole world, all the people. But this truth had to be communicated to the Jewish Christians, including the apostles. While God could have spoken directly, He chose the more indirect method of communication, a dream.

Background: The events of Acts 10–11.

Theme Verse: Acts 10:34–35, "Then Peter opened his mouth and said, 'In truth I perceive that God shows no partiality. But in every nation whoever fears Him and works righteousness is accepted by Him.'"

Reading: Acts 11:1–10, Peter explains the inclusion of the Gentiles.

"Now the apostles and brethren who were in Judea heard that the Gentiles had also received the word of God. And when Peter came up to Jerusalem, those of the circumcision contended with him, saying, 'You went in to uncircumcised men and ate with them!' But Peter explained it to them in order from the beginning, saying: 'I was in the city of Joppa praying; and in a trance I saw a vision, an object descending like a great sheet, let down from heaven by four corners; and it came to me. When I observed it intently and considered, I saw four-footed animals of the earth, wild beasts, creeping things, and birds of the air. And I heard a voice saying to me, 'Rise, Peter; kill and eat.' But I said, 'Not so, Lord! For nothing common or unclean has at any time entered my mouth.' But the voice answered me again from heaven, 'What God has cleansed you must not call common.' Now this was done three times, and all were drawn up again into heaven."

Prayer: Lord Jesus, You extend Your saving grace to all people. May we who love You, love all people in Your name and for Your sake. Through Christ we pray. Amen.

June: The Primitive Church A.D. 30–49

FOURTH WEEK: THE LETTER OF JAMES

Theme: Faith without Works Is Dead

It is thought by many scholars that James is the earliest of the New Testament books, written possibly around A.D. 44. Regardless of the date, James has a message for all Christians that has remained pertinent in every generation: God calls us not only to faith, but also to action. In this day when people are starving, homeless, defenseless, and oppressed, we need, more than ever, to hear God's call through James to put our faith to work.

Background: Acts 15 shows the importance of James in Jerusalem.

Theme Verse: James 2:17, "Faith by itself, if it does not have works, is dead."

Reading: James 1:18–27. James describes a doer.

"Of His own will He brought us forth by the word of truth, that we might be a kind of firstfruits of His creatures. Therefore, my beloved brethren, let every man be swift to hear, slow to speak, slow to wrath; for the wrath of man does not produce the righteousness of God. Therefore lay aside all filthiness and overflow of wicked-ness, and receive with meekness the implanted word, which is able to save your souls. But be doers of the word, and not hearers only, deceiving yourselves. For if anyone is a hearer of the word and not a doer, he is like a man observing his natural face in a mirror; for he observes himself, goes away, and immediately forgets what kind of man he was. But he who looks into the perfect law of liberty and continues in it, and is not a forgetful hearer but a doer of the work, this one will be blessed in what he does. If anyone among you thinks he is religious, and does not bridle his tongue but deceives his own heart, this one's religion is useless. Pure and undefiled religion before God and the Father is this: to visit orphans and widows in their trouble, and to keep oneself unspotted from the world."

Prayer: Lord, we confess it is altogether too easy to listen without acting. Help us not only to know Your will but to do it to Your praise and glory. Receive this our prayer through Jesus Christ. Amen.

July: The Expanding Church A.D. 49–52

FIRST WEEK:
PAUL'S FIRST MISSIONARY JOURNEY

Theme: The Missionary Mandate

I recently gave a talk on modern evangelicalism in a Chicago synagogue. After my speech, a Rabbi who was engaging me in conversation about the differences between the Hebrew faith and the Christian faith, said these words: "I've always thought of my faith as one that is essentially cultural, whereas Christianity is essentially a missionary movement. You Christians are under a mandate to spread your religion." This mandate goes all the way back to the Great Commission which, as we saw last month, goes beyond the Jew to the Gentile. That mission centers around Paul and his missionary journeys, the first of which is our concern for this week.

Background: Read Acts 12:25–14:28.

Theme Verse: Acts 13:2, "As they ministered to the Lord and fasted, the Holy Spirit said, 'Now separate to Me Barnabas and Saul for the work to which I have called them.'"

Reading: Acts 13:42–49. Paul and Barnabas at Antioch of Pisidia.

"And when the Jews went out of the synagogue, the Gentiles begged that these words might be preached to them the next Sabbath. Now when the congregation had broken up, many of the Jews and devout proselytes followed Paul and Barnabas, who, speaking to them, persuaded them to continue in the grace of God. And the next Sabbath almost the whole city came together to hear the word of God. But when the Jews saw the multitudes, they were filled with envy; and contradicting and blaspheming, they opposed the things spoken by Paul. Then Paul and Barnabas grew bold and said, 'It was necessary that the word of God should be spoken to you first;

but since you reject it, and judge yourselves unworthy of everlasting life, behold, we turn to the Gentiles. For so the Lord has commanded us:

'I have set you to be a light to the Gentiles,
That you should be for salvation to the ends of the earth.'

Now when the Gentiles heard this, they were glad and glorified the word of the Lord. And as many as had been appointed to eternal life believed. And the word of the Lord was being spread throughout all the region."

Prayer: Lord, You who sent Paul and Barnabas to the Gentiles, who heard them gladly, grant us courage to proclaim the good news to friends and neighbors. Through Jesus we pray. Amen.

July: The Expanding Church A.D. 49–52

SECOND WEEK: THE LETTER TO THE GALATIANS

Theme: The Purpose of the Law

Many scholars agree that the letter to the Galatian Christians was written after the first missionary journey before Paul left to attend the Jerusalem Council (see Acts 15). Paul wrote the letter to counteract a group of Judaizers who tried to persuade Paul's Gentile converts that it was necessary to become a Jew and keep the Jewish laws as well as believe in Jesus for salvation. Paul insisted in Galatians that the Judaizers were perverting Christianity. The Council of Jerusalem, which met to discuss the matter, set forth a view in agreement with Paul's teaching.

Background: Read Acts 15:1–35 and Galatians.

Theme Verse: Galatians 2:21, "I do not set aside the grace of God; for if righteousness comes through the law, then Christ died in vain."

Reading: Galatians 3:19–25. The purpose of the law.

"What purpose then does the law serve? It was added because of transgressions, till the Seed should come to whom the promise was made; and it was appointed through angels by the hand of a mediator. Now a mediator does not mediate for one only, but God is one. Is the law then against the promises of God? Certainly not! For if there had been a law given which could have given life, truly righteousness would have been by the law. But the Scripture has confined all under sin, that the promise by faith in Jesus Christ might be given to those who believe. But before faith came, we were kept under guard by the law, kept for the faith which would afterward be revealed. Therefore the law was our tutor to bring us to Christ, that we might be justified by faith. But after faith has come, we are no longer under a tutor."

Prayer: Lord, You who gave us the law to lead us to faith, may we trust in Your Son and Him alone for our salvation, we pray. Amen.

July: The Expanding Church A.D. 49–52

THIRD WEEK:
PAUL'S SECOND MISSIONARY JOURNEY

Theme: The Transcultural Nature of the Gospel

On Paul's second missionary journey he went beyond the borders of Asia, up into Greece. In the city of Athens he met and preached to a group of people quite different from those he had met in Asia or in Northern Greece. Here, in this university center of the world, he confronted the philosophers. Apparently, however, his message was not as well received by them as it had been in other parts of the Roman Empire.

Background: Read Acts 15:36–18:22.

Theme Verse: Acts 17:23, "For as I was passing through and considering the objects of your worship, I even found an altar with this inscription: TO THE UNKNOWN GOD. Therefore the One whom you worship without knowing, Him I proclaim to you."

Reading: Acts 17:22–32. Paul's sermon at the Areopagus.

"Then Paul stood in the midst of the Areopagus and said, 'Men of Athens, I perceive that in all things you are very religious; for as I was passing through and considering the objects of your worship, I even found an altar with this inscription: TO THE UNKNOWN GOD.

Therefore, the One whom you worship without know-ing, Him I proclaim to you: God, who made the world and everything in it, since He is the Lord of heaven and earth, does not dwell in temples made with hands. Nor is He worshiped with men's hands, as though He needed anything, since He gives to all life, breath, and all things. And He has made from one blood every nation of men to dwell on all the face of the earth, and has deter-mined their preappointed times and the boundaries of their habitation, so that they should seek the Lord, in the hope that they might grope for Him and find Him, though He is not far from each one of us; for in Him we live and move and have our being, as also some of your own poets have said, "For we are also His offspring." Therefore, since we are the offspring of God, we ought not to think that the Divine Nature is like gold or silver or stone, something shaped by art and man's devising. Truly, these times of ignorance God overlooked, but now commands all men everywhere to repent, because He has appointed a day on which He will judge the world in righteousness by the Man whom He has ordained. He has given assurance of this to all by raising Him from the dead.' And when they heard of the resurrection of the dead, some mocked, while others said, 'We will hear you again on this matter.'"

Prayer: Lord, grant that the word of Your salvation may be heard by all peoples in every culture of the world. Amen.

July: The Expanding Church A.D. 49–52

FOURTH WEEK:
THE LETTERS TO THESSALONICA

Theme: Expecting Christ

During the second missionary journey Paul spent some time preaching and teaching at Thessalonica. Forced to leave, he went on to Corinth, leaving Timothy behind. When Timothy joined him with a report from Thessalonica, he sat down and wrote 1 Thessalonians. Later, a second report prompted Paul to write 2 Thessalonians. Both books address some confusion among these young Christians concerning the second coming of Christ. Paul admonishes them to watch and wait for the return of Christ and to continue going about their daily work and life as they wait for His return.

Background: Acts 17:1–9; 1 and 2 Thessalonians.

Theme Verse: First Thessalonians 5:2, "The day of the Lord so comes as a thief in the night."

Reading: First Thessalonians 4:13–18. The comfort of Christ's coming.

"But I do not want you to be ignorant, brethren, concerning those who have fallen asleep, lest you sorrow as others who have no hope. For if we believe that Jesus died and rose again, even so God will bring with Him those who sleep in Jesus. For this we say to you by the word of the Lord, that we who are alive and remain until the coming of the Lord will by no means precede those who are asleep. For the Lord Himself will descend from heaven with a shout, with the voice of an archangel, and with the trumpet of God. And the dead in Christ will rise first. Then we who are alive and remain shall be caught up together with them in the clouds to meet the Lord in the air. And thus we shall always be with the Lord. Therefore comfort one another with these words."

Prayer: Lord, in watching for Your return, may we live lives of sobriety, pursue what is best for each other, and give thanks to You for all things. Amen.

August: The Expanding Church A.D. 52–58

FIRST WEEK:
PAUL'S THIRD MISSIONARY JOURNEY

Theme: Servanthood

During Paul's missionary journeys a considerable amount of opposition had been building up against him by the Jews who rejected his message. It was rumored among the Christians that the next time Paul went to Jerusalem he would probably be killed or maimed by the Jews who were angry with him. Even in Greece the Jews were so upset with him that they plotted against his life (see Acts 20:3). Before going up to Jerusalem his brethren pleaded with him not to go (see Acts 21:12). In this week's study, Paul, knowing that he will go to Jerusalem and possibly be put to death, gathers the elders of the church at Ephesus for a final farewell.

Background: Read Acts 18:23–21:14.

Theme Verse: Acts 20:24, "But none of these things move me; nor do I count my life dear to myself, so that I may finish my race with joy, and the ministry which I received from the Lord Jesus, to testify to the gospel of the grace of God."

Reading: Acts 20:17–25, 36–38. Paul with the Ephesian elders.

"From Miletus he sent to Ephesus and called for the elders of the church. And when they had come to him, he said to them: 'You know, from the first day that I came to Asia, in what manner I always loved among you, serving the Lord with all humility, with many tears and trials which happened to me by the plotting of the Jews; and how I kept back nothing that was helpful, but proclaimed it to you, and taught you publicly and from house to house, testifying to Jews, and also to Greeks, repentance toward God and faith toward our Lord Jesus Christ. And see, now I go bound in the spirit to Jerusalem, not knowing the things that will happen to me there, except that the Holy Spirit testifies in every city, saying that chains and tribulations await me. But none of these things move me; nor do I count my life dear to myself, so that I may finish my race with joy, and the ministry which I received from the Lord Jesus, to testify to the gospel of the grace of God. And indeed, now I know that you all, among whom I have gone preaching the kingdom of God, will see my face no more.' . . . And when he had said these things, he knelt down and prayed with them all. Then they all wept freely, and fell on Paul's neck and kissed him, sorrowing most of all for the words which he spoke, that they would see his face no more. And they accompanied him to the ship."

Prayer: Lord, grant that we, like Paul, may serve You with joy and gladness all the days of our life. Through Christ we pray. Amen.

Ausust: The Expanding Church A.D. 52–58

SECOND WEEK: 1 CORINTHIANS

Theme: Love

Paul wrote the first letter to the Corinthians during his stay at Ephesus. The letter was stimulated by a report brought through Chloe's household (see 1 Cor. 1:11) that the Christians in Corinth were divided over a number of issues. Paul sent the letter to them by the hand of his close friend and fellow minister, Timothy (see Acts 19:22). It is thought that the outline of 1 Corinthians follows the question presented in the letter brought from Corinth. Paul deals with divisions, marriage, eating food sacrificed to idols, the conduct of worship, the Lord's Supper, spiritual gifts, the resurrection, and collections for the poor. Central to all these issues is the practice of love.

Background: Read Acts 19:1–20:1 and 1 Corinthians.

Theme Verse: First Corinthians 13:1, "Though I speak

with the tongues of men and of angels, but have not love, I have become as sounding brass or a clanging cymbal."

Reading: First Corinthians 13. The greatest gift.

"Though I speak with the tongues of men and of angels, but have not love, I have become as sounding brass or a clanging cymbal. And though I have the gift of prophecy, and understand all mysteries and all knowledge, and though I have all faith, so that I could remove mountains, but have not love, I am nothing. And though I bestow all my goods to feed the poor, and though I give my body to be burned, but have not love, it profits me nothing. Love suffers long and is kind; love does not envy; love does not parade itself, is not puffed up; does not behave rudely, does not seek its own, is not provoked, thinks no evil; does not rejoice in iniquity, but rejoices in the truth; bears all things, believes all things, hopes all things, endures all things. Love never fails. But whether there are prophecies, they will fail; whether there are tongues, they will cease; whether there is knowledge, it will vanish away. For we know in part and we prophesy in part. But when that which is perfect has come, then that which is in part will be done away. When I was a child, I spoke as a child, I understood as a child, I thought as a child; but when I became a man, I put away childish things. For now we see in a mirror, dimly, but then face to face. Now I know in part, but then I shall know just as I also am known. And now abide faith, hope, love, these three; but the greatest of these is love."

Prayer: Lord, grant me the freedom to love others in a truthful and honest way, through Jesus Christ. Amen.

August: The Expanding Church A.D. 52–58

THIRD WEEK: 2 CORINTHIANS

Theme: The New Creation

The evidence is that the Corinthian people were a very hard lot to deal with. Apparently Paul's first letter did not solve their problems and quarrels. There is evidence that Paul wrote them a severe letter against fornication (see 1 Cor. 5:9). And, some argue that he even made a visit from Ephesus to Corinth again, perhaps with the intent of helping them with their problems. On his way Paul met Titus, who brought him a good report of the church in Corinth. Consequently Paul wrote 2 Corinthians from Macedonia expressing his joy over their improved spiritual state. Perhaps that is why he reminded them of their newness in Christ.

Background: Read Acts 19:1–20:1; 2 Corinthians.

Theme Verse: Second Corinthians 5:17, "Therefore, if anyone is in Christ, he is a new creation; old things have passed away; behold, all things have become new."

Reading: Second Corinthians 5:12–21. Be reconciled to God.

"For we do not commend ourselves again to you, but give you opportunity to glory on our behalf, that you may have something to answer those who glory in appearance and not in heart. For if we are beside ourselves, it is for God; or if we are of sound mind, it is for you. For the love of Christ constrains us, because we judge thus: that if One died for all, then all died; and He died for all, that those who live should live no longer for themselves, but for Him who died for them and rose again. Therefore, from now on, we regard no one according to the flesh. Even though we have known Christ according to the flesh, yet now we know Him thus no longer. Therefore, if anyone is in Christ, he is a new creation; old things have passed away; behold, all things have become new. Now all things are of God, who has reconciled us to Himself through Jesus Christ, and has given us the ministry of reconciliation, that is, that God was in Christ reconciling the world to Himself, not imputing their trespasses to them, and has committed to us the word of reconciliation. Therefore we are ambassadors for Christ, as though God were pleading through us: we implore you on Christ's behalf, be reconciled to God. For He made Him who knew no sin to be sin for us, that we might become the righteousness of God in Him."

Prayer: Lord, as You called the Corinthian Christians into newness of life, so You call us to be new creatures. Grant us, Father, the will to be made anew through Jesus our Lord. Amen.

August: The Expanding Church A.D. 52–58

FOURTH WEEK: ROMANS

Theme: Peace with God

It is generally believed that Paul wrote to the Roman Christians while he was in Corinth (see Acts 20:2–3). The theme of Romans is set forth in 1:16–17. Here the gospel is described as the "power of God to salvation for everyone who believes." Paul, in a systematic way, sets forth the gospel by arguing for the world's need (see 1:18–3:20), for justification by faith (see 3:21–8:39); for the peace of the Jew and Gentile in God's plan of salvation (see 9:1–11:36); and then describes the ethical life that grows of the gospel (see 12:1–15:13). He ends with a postscript to his friends (see chap. 16).

Background: Read Acts 20:2–3; Romans.

Theme Verse: Romans 5:1, "Therefore, having been justified by faith, we have peace with God through our Lord Jesus Christ."

Reading: Romans 5:1–11. Faith triumphs over tribulations.

"Therefore, having been justified by faith, we have peace with God through our Lord Jesus Christ, through whom also we have access by faith into this grace in which we stand, and rejoice in hope of the glory of God. And not only that, but we also glory in tribulations, knowing that tribulation produces perseverance; and per-severance, character; and character, hope. Now hope does not disappoint, because the love of God has been poured out in our hearts by the Holy Spirit who was given to us. For when we were still without strength, in due time Christ died for the ungodly. For scarcely a righ-teous man will one die; yet perhaps for a good man some-one would even dare to die. But God demonstrates His own love toward us, in that while we were still sinners, Christ died for us. Much more then, having now been justified by His blood, we shall be saved from wrath through Him. For if when we were enemies we were rec-onciled to God through the death of His Son, much more, having been reconciled, we shall be saved by His life. And not only that, but we also rejoice in God through our Lord Jesus Christ, through whom we have now received the reconciliation."

Prayer: Father, we give You thanks for Your Son through whom we have peace with God. Help us to bring that peace to others, through Jesus Christ our Lord. Amen.

August: The Expanding Church A.D. 52–58

FIFTH WEEK: PAUL'S CAPTURE AND JOURNEY TO ROME

Theme: A Good Conscience

One of Paul's greatest desires was to go to Rome (see Acts 19:21). Little did Paul know that God's plan for him was to go to Rome as a prisoner. At the end of the third missionary journey Paul was seized in Jerusalem and made a prisoner. He defended himself against the Sanhedrin (see Acts 23:1–10), before Felix (see Acts 24:1–27), and before Agrippa (see 25:13–26:31). After spending two years in prison at Caesarea (see Acts 25:4), finally he was sent to Rome (see Acts 27–28), where he remained under house arrest for two more years.

Background: Read Acts 21:15–28:31.

Theme Verse: Acts 23:1, "Men and brethren, I have lived in all good conscience before God until this day."

Reading: Acts 28:23–31.

"So when they had appointed him a day, many came to him at his lodging, to whom he explained and solemnly testified of the kingdom of God, persuading them concerning Jesus from both the Law of Moses and the Prophets, from morning till evening. And some were persuaded by the things which were spoken, and some disbelieved. So when they did not agree among themselves, they departed after Paul had said one word: 'The Holy Spirit spoke rightly through Isaiah the prophet to our fathers, saying,
"Go to this people and say:
'Hearing you will hear, and shall not understand;
And seeing you will see, and not perceive;
For the heart of this people has grown dull.
Their ears are hard of hearing,
And their eyes they have closed,
Lest they should see with their eyes and hear with
their ears,

Let they should understand with their heart and
turn,
So that I should heal them.'"
Therefore let it be known to you that the salvation of
God has been sent to the Gentiles, and they will hear it!'
And when he had said these words, the Jews departed
and had a great dispute among themselves. Then Paul
dwelt two whole years in his own rented house, and re-
ceived all who came to him, preaching the kingdom of
God and teaching the things which concern the Lord
Jesus Christ with all confidence, no one forbidding
him."

Prayer: Father, grant that we, like Paul, may live in good
conscience before You and the world. We pray this
through Jesus our Lord. Amen.

September: Paul's First Imprisonment in Rome A.D. 60–64

FIRST WEEK: EPHESIANS

Theme: The Church

During Paul's two years in the Roman prison he wrote
the letters known to us as the prison epistles: Ephesians,
Colossians, Philippians, and Philemon. Ephesians was a
circular letter written to be read in the churches of Asia.
In Ephesians Paul seems especially concerned with em-
phasizing the oneness of the new churches with Christ
and with each other. The church is the body of Christ
(see 4:15–16), and every believer is a member of His

body (see 1:23; 4:25; 5:23, 30). Consequently, the relationship between Christ and the church is like that of husband to wife (see 5:22–32).

Background: Read Acts 28:30–31 and Ephesians.

Theme Verse: Ephesians 2:19, "Now, therefore, you are no longer strangers and foreigners, but fellow citizens with the saints and members of the household of God."

Reading: Ephesians 5:22–23. Paul instructs the Ephesians.

"Wives, submit to your own husbands, as to the Lord. For the husband is the head of the wife, as also Christ is head of the church; and He is the Savior of the body. Therefore, just as the church is subject to Christ, so let the wives be to their own husbands in everything. Husbands, love your wives, just as Christ also loved the church and gave Himself for it, that He might sanctify and cleanse it with the washing of the water by the word, that He might present it to Himself a glorious church, not having spot or wrinkle or any such thing, but that it should be holy and without blemish. So husbands ought to love their own wives as their own bodies; he who loves his wife loves himself. For no one ever hated his own flesh, but nourishes and cherishes it, just as the Lord does the church. For we are members of His body, of His flesh and of His bones. 'For this reason a man shall leave his father and mother and be joined to his wife, and the two shall become one flesh.' This is a great mystery, but I speak concerning Christ and the church. Nevertheless let each one of you in particular so love his own wife as himself, and let the wife see that she respects her husband."

Prayer: Lord, You called us into community with You and each other in the church. May we love each other even as You love us. Through Christ our Lord we pray. Amen.

September: Paul's First Imprisonment in Rome A.D. 60–64

SECOND WEEK: COLOSSIANS

Theme: The Cosmic Christ

Heresy was not uncommon in the early church. There were always those about who desired to interpret the Christian faith through one or another pagan system. In Colosse some deprived Jesus of His unique status as God and Savior and reduced Him to a mere emanation from God. Paul rejected this teaching and reaffirmed the universal Lordship of Christ. He is the Creator, the One who creates all things and the One who redeems all things.

Background: Read Acts 28:30–31 and Colossians.

Theme Verse: Colossians 3:1, "If then you were raised with Christ, seek those things which are above, where Christ is, sitting at the right hand of God."

Reading: Colossians 1:15–23. Paul affirms the preeminence of Christ.

"He is the image of the invisible God, the firstborn over all creation. For by Him all things were created that are in heaven and that are on earth, visible and invisible, whether thrones or dominions or principalities or powers. All things were created through Him and for Him. And He is before all things, and in Him all things consist. And He is the head of the body, the church, who is the beginning, the firstborn from the dead, that in all things He may have the preeminence. For it pleased the Father that in Him all the fullness should dwell, and by Him to reconcile all things to Himself, by Him, whether things on earth or things in heaven, having made peace through the blood of His cross. And you, who once were alienated and enemies in your mind by wicked works, yet now He has reconciled in the body of His flesh through death, to present you holy, and blameless, and irreproachable in His sight—if indeed you continue in the faith, grounded and steadfast, and are not moved away from the hope of the gospel which you heard, which was preached to every creature under heaven, of which I, Paul, became a minister."

Prayer: Lord Jesus Christ, we acknowledge You to be the Creator, Sustainer, and Redeemer of all that is and is to come. Grant that we should live in this truth through Jesus Christ our Lord. Amen.

September: Paul's First Imprisonment in Rome A.D. 60–64

THIRD WEEK: PHILIPPIANS

Theme: The Mind of Christ

The third of the prison letters was sent by Paul to the Philippians, a small group of Christians who were very close to him. Their relationship was first established during his second missionary journey. And now, more than fifteen years later, Paul wrote to thank them for a gift sent to him in prison (see 4:15–16). While the letter is mainly an expression of Paul's love and joy with an emphasis on practical matters, it does contain a striking hymn on the Incarnation (see 2:5–11). Apparently there was some division in the church between two parties (see 4:2). Paul appeals to them on the basis of the Incarnation to be of the same mind.

Background: Read Acts 28:30–31 and Philippians.

Theme Verse: Philippians 2:5, "Let this mind be in you which was also in Christ Jesus."

Reading: Philippians 2:1–11.

"Therefore if there is any consolation in Christ, if any comfort of love, if any fellowship of the Spirit, if any affection and mercy, fulfill my joy by being like-minded, having the same love, being of one accord, of one mind. Let nothing be done through selfish ambition or conceit, but in lowliness of mind let each esteem others better than himself. Let each of you look out not only for his own interests, but also for the interests of others. Let this mind be in you which was also in Christ Jesus, who, being in the form of God, did not consider it robbery to be equal with God, but made Himself of no reputation, taking the form of a servant, and coming in the likeness of men. And being found in appearance as a man, He humbled Himself and became obedient to the point of death, even the death of the cross. Therefore God also has highly exalted Him and given Him the name which is above every name, that at the name of Jesus every knee should bow, of those in heaven, and of those on earth, and of those under the earth, and that every tongue should confess that Jesus Christ is Lord, to the glory of God the Father."

Prayer: Lord, may the mind of Christ dwell in me; may it shape and mold me into His image, through Jesus Christ I pray. Amen.

September: Paul's First Imprisonment in Rome A.D. 60–64

FOURTH WEEK: PHILEMON

Theme: Brotherly Love

The occasion that prompted the writing of the Philemon epistle was Paul's contact with Onesimus (see v. 10), a runaway slave. Onesimus, who may have stolen something from Philemon, apparently became converted under Paul's ministry. Paul advised him to return to his master and make things right. This brief letter, written from Paul's place of imprisonment in Rome, is a warm and personal letter, revealing the human touch of Paul. Paul begs Philemon to receive him "no longer as a slave but more than a slave, as a beloved brother" (v. 16). It is believed that Paul hoped Philemon would send Onesimus back to Rome to be with Paul as his servant while in prison.

Background: Read Acts 28:30–31 and Philemon.

Theme Verse: Philemon 15–16, "Receive him forever, no longer as a slave but more than a slave, as a beloved brother."

Reading: Philemon 8–16. Paul's plea for Onesimus.

"Therefore, though I might be very bold in Christ to command you what is fitting, yet for love's sake I rather appeal to you—being such a one as Paul, the aged, and now also a prisoner of Jesus Christ—I appeal to you for my son Onesimus, whom I have begotten while in my chains, who once was unprofitable to you, but now is profitable to you and to me. I am sending him back. You therefore receive him, that is, my own heart, whom I wished to keep with me, that on your behalf he might minister to me in my chains for the gospel. But without your consent I wanted to do nothing, that your good deed might not be by compulsion, as it were, but voluntary. For perhaps he departed for a while for this purpose, that you might receive him forever, no longer as a slave but more than a slave, as a beloved brother, especially to me but how much more to you, both in the flesh and in the Lord."

Prayer: Lord, may we, like Philemon, learn to forgive and to receive those who have been restored as our brothers and sisters in Christ, through Christ our Lord. Amen.

October: To Paul's Second Imprisonment in Rome and His Death in A.D. 68

FIRST WEEK: 1 TIMOTHY

Theme: A Qualified Ministry

The two letters 1 Timothy and Titus were written between Paul's two Roman imprisonments, while 2 Timothy was penned when Paul was in prison again, just before his death. A recurrent theme in all these letters is that of guarding the faith. A number of heresies had arisen to threaten orthodoxy, and Paul was concerned lest they should spoil the faithful. Consequently Paul was anxious that a qualified ministry be in place to guard the truth and to hand it over to the next generation. Paul admonishes the Christians to stand fast and not succumb to the heretical teachings.

Background: Read 1 Timothy.

Theme Verse: First Timothy 4:12, "Let no one despise your youth, but be an example to the believers in word, in conduct, in spirit, in faith, in purity."

Reading: First Timothy 3:1–9. Paul states the qualifications of a bishop.

"This is a faithful saying: If a man desires the position of a bishop, he desires a good work. A bishop then must be blameless, the husband of one wife, temperate, sober-minded, of good behavior, hospitable, able to teach; not given to wine, not violent, not greedy for money, but gentle, not quarrelsome, not covetous; one who rules his own house well, having his children in submission with all reverence (for if a man does not know how to rule his own house, how will he take care of the church of God?); not a novice, lest being puffed up with pride he fall into the same condemnation as the devil. Moreover he must have a good testimony among those who are outside, lest he fall into reproach and the snare of the devil. Likewise deacons must be reverent, not double-tongued, not given to much wine, not greedy for money, holding the mystery of the faith with a pure conscience."

Prayer: Father, we give thanks to You for those who minister in Your name. Keep them in Your faith to Your glory. Amen.

October: To Paul's Second Imprisonment in Rome and Death in A.D. 68

SECOND WEEK: TITUS

Theme: Maintain Good Works

Christianity consists of *orthodoxy* and *orthopraxy*. The first refers to the content of the Christian intellectual tradition, the second to the ethical standards of the faith. We are called, in other words, to right belief and right living. Paul was always concerned about both; therefore, his epistles contain teaching on both Christian doctrine and Christian living. In the letter to Titus, these two aspects of the faith are communicated once again.

Background: Read Titus.

Theme Verse: Titus 3:8, "This is a faithful saying, and these things I want you to affirm constantly, that those who have believed in God should be careful to maintain good works."

Reading: Titus 2:11–15; 3:5–7.

"For the grace of God that brings salvation has appeared to all men, teaching us that, denying ungodliness and worldly lusts, we should live soberly, righteously, and godly in the present age, looking for the blessed hope and glorious appearing of our great God and Savior Jesus Christ, who gave Himself for us, that He might redeem us from every lawless deed and purify for Himself His own special people, zealous for good works. Speak these things, exhort, and rebuke with all authority. Let no one despise you. . . . Not by works of righteousness which we have done, but according to His mercy He saved us, through the washing of regeneration and renewing of the Holy Spirit, whom He poured out on us abundantly through Jesus Christ our Savior, that having been justified by His grace we should become heirs according to the hope of eternal life."

Prayer: Father, grant that we Your servants may walk in truth to the glory of Your name. Amen.

October: To Paul's Second Imprisonment in Rome and His Death in A.D. 68

THIRD WEEK: 2 TIMOTHY

Theme: Carry on the Work

When Paul penned his second letter to Timothy he was in jail again, awaiting his death. After several years of freedom he was arrested in Rome. According to tradition he received a martyr's death on the Ostian way, outside of Rome, during the reign of Nero. Knowing that he was soon to die, he was concerned that his work and ministry be carried on. This theme, among others, arises in this letter.

Background: Read 2 Timothy.

Theme Verse: Second Timothy 2:2, "And the things that you have heard from me among many witnesses, commit these to faithful men who will be able to teach others also."

Reading: Second Timothy 3:1–9, 14–17.

"But know this, that in the last days perilous times will come: For men will be lovers of themselves, lovers of money, boasters, proud, blasphemers, disobedient to parents, unthankful, unholy, unloving, unforgiving, slanderers, without self-control, brutal, despisers of good, traitors, headstrong, haughty, lovers of pleasure rather than lovers of God, having a form of godliness but denying its power. And from such people turn away! For of this sort are those who creep into households and make captives of gullible women loaded down with sins, led away by various lusts, always learning and never able to come to the knowledge of the truth. Now as Jannes and Jambres resisted Moses, so do these also resist the truth: men of corrupt minds, disapproved concerning the faith; but they will progress no further, for their folly will be manifest to all, as theirs also was. . . . But as for you, continue in the things which you have learned and been assured of, knowing from whom you have learned them, and that from childhood you have known the Holy Scriptures, which are able to make you wise for salvation through faith which is in Christ Jesus. All Scripture is given by inspiration of God, and is profitable for doctrine, for reproof, for correction, for instruction in righteousness, that the man of God may be complete, thoroughly equipped for every good work."

Prayer: Lord, may we be faithful to Your truth both in what we believe and in the way we live, through Jesus Christ. Amen.

October: To Paul's Second Imprisonment in Rome and His Death in A.D. 68

FOURTH WEEK: 1 PETER

Theme: Suffering in Christ's Name

Christianity was protected from Roman persecution as long as it was regarded as a Jewish sect (Judaism was a recognized religion in Rome). However, when it broke from its Jewish roots and stood alone, it was no longer protected as a legitimate religion. As a nonlegitimate religion it became subject to persecution. The first wave of persecution directed against Christians came during the reign of Nero. Peter wrote his first letter against the background of the Neronian persecution, encouraging the Christians to understand their suffering in light of the suffering of Christ.

Background: Read 1 Peter.

Theme Verse: First Peter 1:7, "That the genuineness of your faith, being much more precious than gold that perishes, though it is tested by fire, may be found to praise, honor, and glory at the revelation of Jesus Christ."

Reading: First Peter 4:12–19.

"Beloved, do not think it strange concerning the fiery trial which is to try you, as though some strange thing happened to you; but rejoice to the extent that you partake of Christ's sufferings, that when His glory is revealed, you may also be glad with exceeding joy. If you are reproached for the name of Christ, blessed are you, for the Spirit of glory and of God rests upon you. On their part He is blasphemed, but on your part He is glorified. But let none of you suffer as a murderer, a thief, an evildoer, or as a busy-body in other people's matters. Yet if anyone suffers as a Christian, let him not be ashamed, but let him glorify God in this matter. For the time has come for judgment to begin at the house of God; and if it begins with us first, what will be the end of those who do not obey the gospel of God? Now 'If the righteous one is scarcely saved,/Where will the ungodly and the sinner appear?' Therefore let those who suffer according to the will of God commit their souls to Him in doing good, as to a faithful Creator."

Prayer: Father, help us to see the connection between our suffering and that of our Lord Jesus Christ. And may we ever be mindful of His love for us, even in the midst of adversity, through Jesus our Lord. Amen.

October: To Paul's Second Imprisonment in Rome and His Death in A.D. 68

FIFTH WEEK: 2 PETER AND JUDE

Theme: Warning against False Prophets

In the latter part of the first century a number of false prophets preached doctrines other than those of the faith. These false prophets created their own theology out of a synthesis of Christianity with pagan ideas. This teaching, known as *Gnosticism* (the word means "higher knowledge"), increasingly became a threat to the Christian faith until the late second century. Both Peter and Jude write against this view and warn the Christians of their time to withstand the idle speculation of a phony gospel.

Background: Read 2 Peter and Jude.

Theme Verse: Jude 3, "I found it necessary to write to

you exhorting you to contend earnestly for the faith which was once for all delivered to the saints."

Reading: Second Peter 2:1–3, 18–20.

"But there were also false prophets among the people, even as there will be false teachers among you, who will secretly bring in destructive heresies, even denying the Lord who bought them, and bring on themselves swift destruction. And many will follow their destructive ways, because of whom the way of truth will be blasphemed. By covetousness they will exploit you with deceptive words; for a long time their judgment has not been idle, and their destruction does not slumber. . . . For when they speak great swelling words of emptiness, they allure through the lusts of the flesh, through licentiousness, the ones who have actually escaped from those who live in error. While they promise them liberty, they themselves are slaves of corruption; for by whom a person is overcome, by him also he is brought into bondage. For if, after they have escaped the pollutions of the world through the knowledge of the Lord and Savior Jesus Christ, they are again entangled in them and overcome, the latter end is worse for them than the beginning."

Prayer: Lord, may we be watchful, guarding against adherence to false interpretations of the faith. Keep us steadfast in Your truth, for Your name's sake. Amen.

November: The Remaining Years to A.D. 100

FIRST WEEK: 1, 2, 3 JOHN

Theme: Love

Paul is known as the apostle of faith, Peter as the apostle of hope, and John as the apostle of love. Although 1 John touches on a number of Christian themes such as the forgiveness of sins, Christian fellowship, the Holy Spirit, and the contrast between light and darkness, love is the overriding theme of John's first letter. Both 2 and 3 John address matters in the church, but the spirit of love that John calls for in 1 John is evident from his pen in these letters also.

Background: Read 1, 2, 3 John.

Theme Verse: First John 4:7, "Beloved, let us love one another, for love is of God; and everyone who loves is born of God and knows God."

Reading: First John 4:7–11, 17–21.

"Beloved, let us love one another, for love is of God; and everyone who loves is born of God and knows God. He who does not love does not know God, for God is love. In this the love of God was manifested toward us, that God has sent His only begotten Son into the world, that we might live through Him. In this is love, not that we loved God, but that He loved us and sent His Son to be the propitiation for our sins. Beloved, if God so loved us, we also ought to love one another. . . . Love has been perfected among us in this: that we may have boldness in the day of judgment; because as He is, so are we in this world. There is no fear in love; but perfect love casts out fear, because fear involves torment. But he who fears has not been made perfect in love. We love Him because He first loved us. If someone says, 'I love God' and hates his brother, he is a liar; for he who does not love his brother whom he has seen, how can he love God whom he has not seen? And this commandment we have from Him: that he who loves God must love his brother also."

Prayer: Lord Jesus Christ, You have shown us how to love. Grant that we may follow Your example and live by the rule of love. Through Jesus Christ our Lord we pray. Amen.

November: The Remaining Years to A.D. 100

SECOND WEEK: HEBREWS

Theme: Endurance

The book of Hebrews was written to Jewish Christians who were tempted to turn away from the Christian faith and return to Judaism. The unknown author argues for the superiority of the Christian faith. Christ is superior to the prophets, angels, Moses, Joshua, and the Aaronic priesthood. It is a better covenant (see 6:9) that God has established with His new people. On this basis the recipients are urged again and again to remain steadfast in the gospel.

Background: Read the entire epistle to the Hebrews.

Theme Verse: Hebrews 3:14, "We have become partakers of Christ if we hold the beginning of our confidence steadfast to the end."

Reading: Hebrews 6:1–6, 9–15.

"Therefore, leaving the discussion of the elementary principles of Christ, let us go on to perfection, not laying again the foundation of repentance from dead works and of faith toward God, of the doctrine of baptisms, of laying on of hands, of resurrection of the dead, and of eternal judgment. And this we will do if God permits. For it is impossible for those who were once enlightened, and have tasted the heavenly gift, and have become partakers of the Holy Spirit, and have tasted the good word of God and the powers of the age to come, if they fall away, to renew them again to repentance, since they crucify again for themselves the Son of God, and put Him to an open shame. . . . But, beloved, we are confident of better things concerning you, yes, things that accompany salvation, though we speak in this manner. For God is not unjust to forget your work and labor of love which you have shown toward His name, in that you have ministered to the saints, and do minister. And we desire that each one of you show the same diligence to the full assurance of hope until the end, that you do not become sluggish, but imitate those who through faith and patience inherit the promises. For when God made a promise to Abraham, because He could swear by no one greater, He swore by Himself, saying, 'Surely blessing I will bless you, and multiplying I will multiply you.' And so, after he had patiently endured, he obtained the promise."

Prayer: Lord, may we, like Abraham, endure to the end. And grant us, heavenly Father, life everlasting through Your Son Jesus Christ. Amen.

November: The Remaining Years to A.D. 100

THIRD WEEK: REVELATION: THE STATE OF THE CHURCH AT THE END OF THE FIRST CENTURY

Theme: Images of the Church

Throughout history the church has been strong and weak, dead and alive, viable and lethargic. In the early chapters of Revelation, the last of the New Testament books, we gain an insight into the various conditions of the church at that time. Some, like Ephesus, had lost their first love; others, like Pergamos, were characterized by false teaching. These images of the church stand as a prophetic reminder to us today to remain true to our calling in Christ Jesus.

Background: Read Revelation 2–3.

Theme Verse: Revelation 2:7, "He who has an ear, let him hear what the Spirit says to the churches."

Reading: Revelation 3:7–13.

"And to the angel of the church in Philadelphia write, 'These things says He who is holy, He who is true, "He who has the key of David, He who opens and no one shuts, and shuts and no one opens": I know your works. See, I have set before you an open door, and no one can shut it; for you have a little strength, have kept My word, and have not denied My name. Indeed I will make those of the synagogue of Satan, who say they are Jews and are not, but lie—indeed I will make them come and worship before your feet, and to know that I have loved you. Because you have kept My command to persevere, I also will keep you from the hour of trial which shall come upon the whole world, to test those who dwell on the earth. Behold, I come quickly! Hold fast what you have, that no one may take your crown. He who overcomes, I will make him a pillar in the temple of My God, and he shall go out no more. And I will write on him the name of My God and the name of the city of My God, the New Jerusalem, which comes down out of heaven from My God. And I will write on him My new name. He who has an ear, let him hear what the Spirit says to the churches.'"

Prayer: Lord, You have given us, the church, the privilege of proclaiming Your name throughout the world. May we be faithful to Your calling in word and deed. Through Christ our Lord. Amen.

November: The Remaining Years to A.D. 100

FOURTH WEEK: REVELATION: THE HOPE OF THE CHURCH

Theme: The New Heavens and the New Earth

The Scriptures sweep from the beginning of the world to the end, from creation to eschatology. What begins with "In the beginning God created the heavens and the earth" (Gen. 1:1) ends with "I saw a new heaven and a new earth" (Rev. 21:1). Between the covers of the Bible is the story of the universe, the story of humanity. For although we fell away into sin and corrupted the earth with evil, God in Jesus Christ has restored us and His creation to Himself. Thus, the Bible ends on this optimistic note of praise.

Background: Read Revelation 4–22.

Theme Verse: Revelation 21:1, "I saw a new heaven and a new earth, for the first heaven and the first earth had passed away."

Reading: Revelation 21:10–11, 23–26; 22:1–5.

"And he carried me away in the Spirit to a great and high mountain, and showed me the great city, the holy Jerusalem, descending out of heaven from God, having the glory of God. And her light was like a most precious stone, like a jasper stone, clear as crystal. . . . And the city had no need of the sun or of the moon to shine in it,

271

for the glory of God illuminated it, and the Lamb is its light. And the nations of those who are saved shall walk in its light, and the kings of the earth bring their glory and honor into it. Its gates shall not be shut at all by day (there shall be no night there). And they shall bring the glory and the honor of the nations into it. . . . And he showed me a pure river of water of life, clear as a crystal, proceeding from the throne of God and of the Lamb. In the middle of its street, and on either side of the river, was the tree of life, which bore twelve fruits, each tree yielding its fruit every month. And the leaves of the tree were for the healing of the nations. And there shall be no more curse, but the throne of God and of the Lamb shall be in it, and His servants shall serve Him. They shall see His face, and His name shall be on their foreheads. And there shall be no night there: They need no lamp nor light of the sun, for the Lord God gives them light. And they shall reign forever and ever."

Prayer: Lord, grant that we Your people should live always aware of the vision of the future. Blessed be Your name. Amen.

PART III

Family Prayers for Special Occasions

THE FAMILY Man with his wife and children

INTRODUCTION TO
Family Prayers for Special Occasions

A few years ago my family and I were being enter-
tained on Thanksgiving Day at the home of relatives.
Other relatives from the area were there as well. And
since we drove more than a thousand miles to be present
with relatives whom we see infrequently, the gathering
had a special joyous and happy flavor to it.

When my sister-in-law called us all to the table, she
made a remark that I will never forget. Here we were,
eight adults and ten children all dressed in our finest
clothes. We were standing around the table which was
decked out with fine china, silverware, and goblets. On
the table was the turkey, stuffing, potatoes, vegetables,
and salad. It was obvious that considerable attention had
been given to the preparation of this event. And now it
was time to say the blessing before the enjoyment of the
meal. As we stood there at our places, my sister-in-law
said, "Oh, I wish we had prepared a service."

The family prayers of this section are intended to
fulfill the desire expressed by my sister-in-law. I am sure
many Christian people, after having spent hours prepar-

ing a meal for a special occasion such as a birthday, an anniversary, a retirement, or Mother's Day, have longed for a meaningful Christian context in which that meal could be celebrated. These prayers are designed to satisfy that longing and to sanctify the occasion. They may be used either before or after the meal. In some cases part of the prayers are before the meal, with others coming after the meal.

ON THE OCCASION OF
THE BIRTH OF A CHILD

Leader: We gather today in the spirit of rejoicing to celebrate the birth of *(name)*. Let us bless the name of God who has brought this child into our home. Hear the word of the Lord from Matthew: "Let the little children come to me, and do not forbid them; for of such is the kingdom of heaven" (19:14).

Let us pray.

Father, we thank You for the life of this little one. May Your blessing be upon *(her/him)*. Cause this child to grow in wisdom, and grant that we may provide a home of love and warmth, through Jesus Christ our Lord. Amen.

The Scripture Reading

First Reader: A reading from the book of Psalms: "I will praise You with my whole heart;

Before the gods I will sing praises to You.
I will worship toward Your holy temple,
And praise Your name
For Your lovingkindness and Your truth;
For You have magnified Your word above all
    Your name.
In the day when I cried out, You answered
    me,
And made me bold with strength in my soul.
All the kings of the earth shall praise You, O
    LORD,
When they hear the words of Your mouth.
Yes, they shall sing of the ways of the LORD,
For great is the glory of the LORD" (138:1–5).

This is the word of the Lord.

Response: Thanks be to God.

Second   A reading from the gospel according to Luke:
Reader: "Now there were in the same country shepherds living out in the fields, keeping watch
over their flock by night. And behold, an angel of the Lord stood before them, and the
glory of the Lord shone around them, and
they were greatly afraid. Then the angel said
to them, 'Do not be afraid, for behold, I bring
you good tidings of great joy which will be to
all people. For there is born to you this day in
the city of David a Savior, who is Christ the
Lord. And this will be a sign to you: You will
find a Babe wrapped in swaddling clothes,
lying in a manger.' And suddenly there was
with the angel a multitude of the heavenly

host praising God and saying: 'Glory to God in the highest,/And on earth peace, good will toward men!'" (2:8–14).

This is the word of the Lord.

Response: Thanks be to God.

The Prayer of Dedication

Leader: Let us dedicate this child to the Lord. Gracious Father, You have taught us, through Jesus Your Son, that those who receive a child in Your name receive Christ Himself. We give thanks to You for the blessings You have granted through the birth of this child. May this child be brought up in the nurture of the faith, and may all that is good and true, especially lively faith in Jesus Christ, be this child's portion. We pray this in the name of Jesus Christ our Lord. Amen.

(Here the feast of joy may commence.)

ON THE OCCASION OF A BAPTISM

Leader: Dear family and friends, baptism is the glorious symbol of God's love for us and of our response to Him. We gather under the sign of baptism today to celebrate the baptism of (*name*). Let us rejoice in the God who saves us and in the faith here affirmed.

Let us pray.

Lord, You have given us water as a sign of the new creation. Grant that this sign of Your grace may be met by the soul's desire and bring us all to Your glory, through Christ our Lord. Amen.

The Scripture Readings

First Reader: A reading from Romans:

"Or do you not know that as many of us as were baptized into Christ Jesus were baptized into His death? Therefore we were buried with Him through baptism into death, that just as Christ was raised from the dead by the glory of the Father, even so we also should walk in newness of life. For if we have been united together in the likeness of His death, certainly we also shall be in the likeness of His resurrection, knowing this, that our old man was crucified with Him, that the body of sin might be done away with, that we should no longer be slaves of sin" (6:3–6).

This is the word of the Lord.

Response: Thanks be to God.

Second Reader: A reading from Colossians:

"If then you were raised with Christ, seek those things which are above, where Christ is, sitting at the right hand of God. Set your mind on things above, not on things on the earth. For you died, and your life is hidden with Christ in God. . . . Therefore, as the elect of God, holy and beloved, put on tender mercies, kindness, humbleness of mind, meekness, longsuffering; bearing with one another, and forgiving one another, if anyone has a complaint against another; even as Christ forgave you, so you also must do. But above all these things put on love, which is the bond of perfection. And let the peace of God rule in your hearts, to which also you were called in one body; and be thankful. Let the word of Christ dwell in you richly in all wisdom, teaching and admonishing one another in psalms and hymns and spiritual songs, singing with grace in your hearts to the Lord. And whatever you do in word or deed, do all in the name of the Lord Jesus, giving thanks to God the Father through Him" (3:1–3, 12–17).

This is the word of the Lord.

Response: Thanks be to God.

Affirming the Covenant

Leader: In the early church it was the custom for all people to reaffirm their covenant at every baptism. Therefore, in the following words, we will reaffirm our faith and our commitment:

Do you believe in God the Father?

Response: I believe in God, the Father almighty, creator of heaven and earth.

Leader: Do you believe in Jesus Christ, the Son of God?

Response: I believe in Jesus Christ, His only Son, our Lord. He was conceived by the power of the Holy Spirit and born of the Virgin Mary. He suffered under Pontius Pilate, was crucified, died, and was buried. He descended to the dead. On the third day He rose again. He ascended into heaven, and is seated at the right hand of the Father. He will come again to judge the living and the dead.

Leader: Do you believe in God the Holy Spirit?

Response: I believe in the Holy Spirit, the holy catholic church, the communion of saints, the forgiveness of sins, the resurrection of the body, and life everlasting.

Leader: Will you continue in the apostles' teaching and fellowship, in the breaking of bread, and in the prayers? If so, answer, "I will, with God's help."

Response: I will, with God's help.

Leader: Will you persevere in resisting evil, and, whenever you fall into sin, repent and return to the Lord?

Response: I will, with God's help.

Leader: Will you proclaim by word and example the Good News of God in Christ?

Response: I will, with God's help.

Leader: Will you seek and serve Christ in all persons, loving your neighbor as yourself?

Response: I will, with God's help.

Leader: Will you strive for justice and peace among all people, and respect the dignity of every human being?

Response: I will, with God's help.

The Prayer of Commitment

Leader: Father, we who are gathered here today rejoice in the baptism of (*name*), and with (*him/ her*) we reaffirm our baptismal vows. Deliver us, O Lord, from the way of death. Open our hearts to Your faith. Fill us with Your life-giving spirit. Keep us in Your holy church, and grant us the power to live in our vows, through Jesus our Lord and Savior. Amen.

The Dismissal

Leader: Let us greet the baptized with the kiss of peace.
(*Here each may greet the baptized with a hand-shake or an appropriate hug, saying, "The Peace of the Lord be with you." In the case of an infant the greeting may be extended to the parents.*)

ON THE OCCASION
OF INFANT DEDICATION

Leader: Dear family and friends, God has seen fit to bring the infant (*name*) into the world. Let us rejoice together in the dedication of this child to the Lord, and let us pray together for (*his/ her*) spiritual health and growth.

Let us pray.

Father, Your Son, the Lord Jesus, welcomed the children into His kingdom. Protect, we pray, this child and bring (*him/her*) into a saving relationship with Your Son, and into fellowship with Your church, the body of Christ. We pray through Jesus our Lord. Amen.

The Scripture Readings

First   A reading from Luke:
Reader: "And behold, there was a man in Jerusalem whose name was Simeon, and this man was just and devout, waiting for the Consolation of Israel, and the Holy Spirit was upon him. And it had been revealed to him by the Holy Spirit that he would not see death before he had seen the Lord's Christ. So he came by the Spirit into the temple. And when the parents brought in the Child Jesus, to do for Him according to the custom of the law, he took Him up in his arms and blessed God and said:

'Lord, now You are letting Your servant depart
in peace,
According to Your word;
For my eyes have seen Your salvation
Which You have prepared before the face of
all peoples,
A light to bring revelation to the Gentiles,
And the glory of Your people Israel.'
And Joseph and His mother marveled at those
things which were spoken of Him"
(2:25–33).

This is the word of the Lord.

Response: Thanks be to God.

**Second
Reader:** A reading from 2 Timothy:
"I thank God, whom I serve with a pure conscience, as my forefathers did, as without
ceasing I remember you in my prayers night
and day, greatly desiring to see you, being
mindful of your tears, that I may be filled with
joy, when I call to remembrance the genuine
faith that is in you, which dwelt first in your
grandmother Lois and your mother Eunice,
and I am persuaded is in you also. Therefore I
remind you to stir up the gift of God which
is in you through the laying on of my hands.
For God has not given us a spirit of fear, but
of power and of love and of a sound mind"
(1:3–7).

This is the word of the Lord.

Response: Thanks be to God.

The Prayer of Commitment

Leader: Let us commit the life of (*name*) to the Lord. Lord Jesus, we bring (*name*) to You. For You alone are Lord of the universe. We confess that You are the Lord of (*name*)'s life. We commit (*his/her*) life into Your hands, and we pray You grant the will and wisdom needed to bring this child up in the fear and admonition of the Lord and in the fellowship of the church, Your body.

Response: Amen.

(*Here the festivities may commence.*)

ON THE OCCASION
OF A CONFIRMATION

Leader: Dear family and friends, today is a very special day in the life of (*name*); for on this day (*she/he*) has made a public commitment to the intent of baptism. (*Name*) has affirmed (*his/her*) personal faith in Jesus Christ as Lord and Savior. Together with the angels we gather to celebrate this glorious occasion.

Let us pray.

Lord God, we bless You for Your continued presence in the life of (*name*). Grant that the work that You have begun in (*his/her*) life will be maintained until that day when we all shall gather at the feet of Jesus Your Son, in whose name we pray.

Response: Amen.

The Scripture Reading

First Reader: A reading from Paul's letter to the Ephesians: "Blessed be the God and Father of our Lord Jesus Christ, who has blessed us with every spiritual blessing in the heavenly places in Christ, just as he chose us in Him before the foundation of the world, that we should be holy and without blame before Him in love, having predestined us to adoption as sons by Jesus Christ to Himself, according to the good pleasure of His will, to the praise of the glory of His grace, by which He has made us accepted in the Beloved. In Him we have redemption through His blood, the forgiveness of sins, according to the riches of His grace which He made to abound toward us in all wisdom and prudence, having made known to us the mystery of His will, according to His good pleasure which He purposed in Himself, that in the dispensation of the fullness of the times He might gather together in one all things in Christ, both which are in heaven and which are on earth—in Him, in whom also we have obtained an inheritance, being predestined according to the purpose of Him who works all things according to the counsel of His will, that we who first trusted in Christ should be to the praise of His glory. In Him you also trusted, after you heard the word of truth, the gospel of your salvation; in whom also, having believed, you were sealed with the Holy Spirit of promise" (1:3–13).

This is the word of the Lord.

Response: Thanks be to God.

The Words of Admonition

Leader: I invite all who are here present to offer a brief word of wisdom to (*name*). (*One or more may speak.*) At the conclusions of each speech, all shall say "Amen!"

The Prayer of Commitment

Leader: Let us give thanks for the confirmation of (*name*).

Almighty God, by the glorious death and resurrection of Your Son, You have put to flight the power of evil. Bless now (*name*), who has been sealed in Your Spirit. Send (*him/her*) and us forth in the power of Your Spirit to perform Your service, to lighten the paths of others, to glorify Your name, through Jesus our Lord.

Response: Amen.

(*Here the festivities may commence.*)

ON THE OCCASION OF A BIRTHDAY

Leader: My dear friends, today is a special day in the life of our family, for on this day we celebrate the birth of (*name*). Let us begin by giving thanks to God Almighty.

Let us pray.

Father, we praise You for every perfect gift that comes from above. You have gifted us with the life of (*name*). Now we bless You for (*his/her*) presence in our family. Grant, we pray You, that Your blessing may rest upon (*him/her*) all the days of (*his/her*) life. Amen.

The Scripture Readings

First Reader: A Reading from Ecclesiastes:
"To everything there is a season.
A time for every purpose under heaven:
A time to be born,
   And a time to die;
A time to plant,
   And a time to pluck what is planted;
A time to kill,
   And a time to heal;
A time to break down,
   And a time to build up;
A time to weep,
   And a time to laugh;

A time to mourn,
   And a time to dance;
A time to cast away stones,
   And a time to gather stones;
A time to embrace,
   And a time to refrain from embracing;
A time to gain,
   And a time to lose;
A time to keep,
   And a time to throw away;
A time to tear,
   And a time to sew;
A time to keep silence,
   And a time to speak;
A time to love,
   And a time to hate;
A time of war,
   And a time of peace" (Eccles. 3:1–8).

This is the word of the Lord.

Response: Thanks be to God.

Second Reader: A reading from the gospel according to John: "There was a man of the Pharisees named Nicodemus, a ruler of the Jews. This man came to Jesus by night and said to Him, 'Rabbi, we know that You are a teacher come from God; for no one can do these signs that You do unless God is with him.' Jesus answered and said to him, 'Most assuredly, I say to you, unless one is born again, he cannot see the kingdom of God.' Nicodemus said to Him, 'How can a man be born when he is old?

Can he enter a second time into his mother's womb and be born?' Jesus answered, 'Most assuredly, I say to you, unless one is born of water and the Spirit, he cannot enter the kingdom of God. That which is born of the flesh is flesh, and that which is born of the Spirit is spirit. Do not marvel that I said to you, "You must be born again." The wind blows where it wishes, and you hear the sound of it, but cannot tell where it comes from and where it goes. So is everyone who is born of the Spirit'" (3:1–8).

This is the word of the Lord.

Response: Thanks be to God.

The Presentation of Gifts

(The gifts may now be brought.)

Leader: *(Name),* these gifts are tokens of the love and esteem we have for you. Before you open them, we wish to express our love to you in words. Each of us has thought of something about you that we appreciate. We want to acknowledge you in this way. *(Each person may now state a positive characteristic of the person whose birth is being celebrated by saying: I like ———or I appreciate———.)*

The Prayer of Dedication

Leader: Let us dedicate *(name)* to the Lord.
Father, we dedicate *(name)* to Your service.

We ask that (*his/her*) life may bring glory to Your name, through Jesus Christ our Lord.

Response: Amen.

(*The gifts may now be opened and the cake shared by all.*)

ON THE OCCASION OF AN ENGAGEMENT (BETROTHAL)

Leader: Dear family and friends, we have gathered on this occasion to honor (*name*) and (*name*), who have announced their intention to unite in holy marriage. This is a festive and wonderful moment in their lives and ours; so let us be festive and rejoice.

Let us pray.

Lord God, You bring to pass all things under Your providence. In Your holy wisdom You have seen fit to bring (*name*) and (*name*) into a loving relationship. In this celebration of their intent, we praise You for Your hand in their lives. As You have been present to them in the past, be with them now and throughout their life together, in Jesus' name we pray. Amen.

The Scripture Readings

First Reader: A reading from Genesis:

"And the LORD God said, 'It is not good that

man should be alone; I will make him a helper comparable to him.' Out of the ground the LORD God formed every beast of the field and every bird of the air, and brought them to Adam to see what he would call them. And whatever Adam called each living creature, that was its name. So Adam gave names to all cattle, to the birds of the air, and to every beast of the field. But for Adam there was not found a helper comparable to him. And the LORD God caused a deep sleep to fall on Adam, and he slept; and He took one of his ribs, and closed up the flesh in its place. Then the rib which the LORD God had taken from man He made into a woman, and He brought her to the man. And Adam said:
'This is now bone of my bones
And flesh of my flesh;
She shall be called Woman,
Because she was taken out of Man.'
Therefore a man shall leave his father and mother and be joined to his wife, and they shall become one flesh" (2:18–24).

This is the word of the Lord.

Response: Thanks be to God.

Second Reader: A reading from the First Epistle of John: "Beloved, let us love one another, for love is of God; and everyone who loves is born of God and knows God. He who does not love does not know God, for God is love. In this the love of God was manifested toward us, that

God has sent His only begotten Son into the world, that we might live through Him. In this is love, not that we loved God, but that He loved us and sent His Son to be the propitiation for our sins. Beloved, if God so loved us, we also ought to love one another. No one has seen God at any time. If we love one another, God abides in us, and His love has been perfected in us. By this we know that we abide in Him, and He in us, because He has given us of His Spirit. And we have seen and testify that the Father has sent the Son as Savior of the world. Whoever confesses that Jesus is the Son of God, God abides in him, and he in God. And we have known and believed the love that God has for us. God is love, and he who abides in love abides in God, and God in him" (4:7–16).

This is the word of the Lord.

Response: Thanks be to God.

Words of Advice and Admonition

Leader: (*Name*) and (*name*), we wish to congratulate you and offer words of wisdom and advice from our experience. I invite those who have a word for your direction in life to speak now.

(*Here as many as wish may make appropriate comments.*)

Prayer of Commitment

Leader: Let us pray for (*name*) and (*name*).

Lord, from You love originates, from everlasting You. Father, Son, and Holy Spirit have been bound together in love. You bestowed love upon Your creation. You poured out Your love in Jesus Christ. Now, O source of love, grant that (*name*) and (*name*) shall love You and each other more and more, through Christ our Lord.

Response: Amen.

(Here may follow the opening of gifts and festive celebration of the engagement.)

ON THE OCCASION OF A WEDDING

(For the Bridal Dinner or Reception)

Leader: Dear friends, today is a most happy occasion; for on this day we celebrate the marriage of (*name*) and (*name*). We believe God has called them to live together in holy matrimony, so we gather to give them our support and to wish them well.

Let us pray.

Lord God, You who adorn the sky with clouds and stars, You who beautify the earth with shrubs and flowers, grant that the marriage of (*name*) and (*name*) may be sanctified by Your grace, to Your glory and their enjoyment, we pray. Amen.

The Scripture Readings

First Reader: A reading from the Song of Solomon:
"My beloved spoke, and said to me;
'Rise up, my love, my fair one,
And come away.
For lo, the winter is past,
The rain is over and gone.
The flowers appear on the earth;
The time of singing has come,
And the voice of the turtledove
Is heard in our land.
The fig tree puts forth her green figs,
And the vines with the tender grapes
Give a good smell.
Rise up, my love, my fair one,
And come away!
O my dove, in the clefts of the rock,
In the secret places of the cliff,
Let me see your countenance,
Let me hear your voice;
For your voice is sweet,
And your countenance is lovely.' . . .
Many waters cannot quench love,
Nor can the floods drown it.
If a man would give for love
All the wealth of his house,
It would be utterly despised"
(2:10–14; 8:7).

This is the word of the Lord.

Response: Thanks be to God.

Second Reader: A reading from the First Epistle of John: "Beloved, let us love one another, for love is of God; and everyone who loves is born of God and knows God. He who does not love does not know God, for God is love. In this the love of God was manifested toward us, that God has sent His only begotten Son into the world, that we might live through Him. In this is love, not that we loved God, but that He loved us and sent His Son to be the propitiation for our sins. Beloved, if God so loved us, we also ought to love one another. No one has seen God at any time. If we love one another, God abides in us, and His love has been perfected in us. By this we know that we abide in Him, and He in us, because He has given us of His spirit. And we have seen and testify that the Father has sent the Son as Savior of the world. Whoever confesses that Jesus is the Son of God, God abides in him, and he in God. And we have known and believed the love that God has for us. God is love, and he who abides in love abides in God, and God in him" (4:7–16).

This is the word of the Lord.

Response: Thanks be to God.

The Feast

> (*If a feast is part of the celebration, it may take place here after the prayer.*)

Leader: Let us give thanks to God for this food.
Lord God, we acknowledge You as the giver of all good things. Bless this food to our enjoyment. May we feast together, celebrating Your presence with us and with this marriage, through Christ our Lord. Amen.

The Final Prayers

> (*After the meal or reception, the leader may say:*)

Leader: Let us send (*name*) and (*name*) forth in prayer:
Lord of heaven and earth, grant Your servants (*name*) and (*name*) journeying mercies on their honeymoon. Bestow upon them love for each other and for You, And bring them and us to Your eternal kingdom, through Jesus Christ our Lord.

Response: Amen.

ON THE OCCASION OF A WEDDING ANNIVERSARY

Leader: We have gathered this day to celebrate the anniversary of (*name*) and (*name*). We give thanks to God that they were brought together in holy matrimony (*number*) years ago, and we offer special thanks to the Father who has granted grace to them over the years.

Let us pray.

Father in heaven, we praise You for the marriage of (*name*) and (*name*), and we bless You for the witness of their life and love. Grant, O heavenly One, that they may be blessed with continued love and happiness together, through Jesus Christ our Lord. Amen.

The Scripture Readings

First   A reading from Genesis:
Reader: "And the LORD God said, 'It is not good that man should be alone; I will make him a helper comparable to him.' . . . And the LORD God caused a deep sleep to fall on Adam, and he slept; and He took one of his ribs, and closed up the flesh in its place. Then the rib which the LORD God had taken from man He made into a woman, and He brought her to the man. And Adam said:
'This now is bone of my bones
And flesh of my flesh;
She shall be called Woman,
Because she was taken out of Man.'
Therefore a man shall leave his father and mother and be joined to his wife, and they shall become one flesh" (2:18, 21–24).

This is the word of the Lord.

Response: Thanks be to God.

299

**Second
Reader:** A reading from the gospel according to John: "On the third day there was a wedding in Cana of Galilee, and the mother of Jesus was there. Now both Jesus and His disciples were invited to the wedding. And when they ran out of wine, the mother of Jesus said to Him, 'They have no wine.' Jesus said to her, 'Woman, what does your concern have to do with Me? My hour has not yet come.' His mother said to the servants, 'Whatever He says to you, do it.' Now there were set there six waterpots of stone, according to the manner of purification of the Jews, containing twenty or thirty gallons apiece. Jesus said to them, 'Fill the waterpots with water.' And they filled them up to the brim. And He said to them, 'Draw some out now, and take it to the master of the feast.' And they took it. When the master of the feast had tasted the water that was made wine, and did not know where it came from (but the servants who had drawn the water knew), the master of the feast called the bridegroom. And he said to him, 'Every man at the beginning sets out the good wine, and when the guests have well drunk, then that which is inferior; but you have kept the good wine until now.' This beginning of signs Jesus did in Cana of Galilee, and manifested His glory; and His disciples believed in Him" (2:1–11).

This is the word of the Lord.

Response: Thanks be to God.

The Re-enactment of Vows

Leader: (*Name*) and (*name*) will now repeat their vows as a sign of their continuing love and fidelity to each other.

Husband: It is my will to continue to have you as my wife, and to live with you in the covenant of marriage. I will continue to love you, comfort you, honor and keep you, in sickness and in health; and continuing to forsake all others, I pledge you my faithfulness as long as we live.

Wife: It is my will to continue to have you as my husband and to live with you in the covenant of marriage. I will continue to love you, comfort you, honor and keep you, in sickness and in health, and continuing to forsake all others, to be faithful to you as long as we both live.

The Prayer of Rededication

Leader: Let us rededicate (*name*) and (*name*) in marriage.
Father Almighty, in Your divine providence You have willed to bring (*name*) and (*name*) together in holy matrimony. In this day when marriage is beset by stress, we pray for Your special grace. Keep their love strong, their commitment steadfast; and may their joy increase more and more, through Jesus Christ our Lord. Amen.

Celebrating the Marriage

Leader: Having witnessed the re-enactment of these vows, let us now toast (*name*) and (*name*) with words of encouragement. I ask each of you to speak a word of encouragement or make reference to something from their life that has been of special help to you.

(*Those who wish may make appropriate comments.*)

The peace of the Lord be with you.

Response: And also with you.

(*Greet each other with a handshake or an appropriate hug, saying, "The Peace of the Lord be with you."*)

ON THE OCCASION OF
A RETIREMENT.

Leader: My dear friends, today we have gathered to celebrate the work of our dear friend (*name*) and to welcome (*his/her*) deserved rest from the daily demands of (*his/her*) work. Let us rejoice in God who has given us work to do, and let us be reminded of the promise of Sabbath rest.

Let us pray.

Father Almighty, in six days You created the world, and on the seventh You rested. You, who are known by Your works, are the Lord of life and work. We bless You for the work of (*name*). Now grant (*him/her*) rest in the activities of retirement, through Jesus Christ our Lord. Amen.

The Scripture Readings

First
Reader: A reading from Genesis:
"The LORD God planted a garden eastward in Eden, and there He put the man whom He had formed. And out of the ground the LORD God made every tree grow that is pleasant to the sight and good for food. The tree of life was also in the midst of the garden, and the tree of knowledge of good and evil. Now a river went out of Eden to water the garden, and from there it parted and became four riverheads. The name of the first is Pishon; it is the one which encompasses the whole land of Havilah, where there is gold. And the gold of that land is good. Bdellium and onyx stone are there. The name of the second river is Gihon; it is the one which encompasses the whole land of Cush. The name of the third river is Hiddekel; it is the one which goes toward the east of Assyria. The fourth river is the Euphrates. Then the LORD God took the man and put him in the garden of Eden to tend and keep it" (2:8–15).

This is the word of the Lord.

Response: Thanks be to God.

Second   A reading from Hebrews:
Reader: "Therefore, since a promise remains of entering His rest, let us fear lest any of you seem to
have come short of it. For indeed the gospel
was preached to us as well as to them; but the
word which they heard did not profit them,
not being mixed with faith in those who
heard it. For we who have believed do enter
that rest, as He has said: 'So I swore in My
wrath,/They shall not enter My rest,' although the works were finished from the
foundation of the world. For He has spoken in
a certain place of the seventh day in this way;
'And God rested on the seventh day from all
His works'; and again in this place: 'They shall
not enter My rest.' Since therefore it remains
that some must enter it, and those to whom it
was first preached did not enter because of dis-
obedience, again He designates a certain day,
saying in David, 'Today,' after such a long
time, as it has been said: 'Today, if you will
hear His voice,/Do not harden your hearts.'
For if Joshua had given them rest, then He
would not afterward have spoken of another
day. There remains therefore a rest for the
people of God. For he who has entered His
rest has himself also ceased from his works as
God did from His" (4:1–10).

This is the word of the Lord.

Response: Thanks be to God.

Testimonials

Leader: We now wish to express our appreciation to (*name*) for (*his/her*) work and to wish (*him/her*) well in the future.

(*Those who have asked to make speeches may do so at this time.*)

The Prayer of Dedication

Leader: Let us dedicate (*name*) to the Lord. Father, as there is a time to work and labor and a time to rest, grant that the rest into which (*name*) enters may be filled with the joy of life. Protect (*his/her*) coming and going, fill (*his/her*) life with friendships, bless (*him/her*) with health, and grant (*him/her*) peace, through Jesus Christ our Lord we pray. Amen.

(*Friends may now gather to congratulate and offer best wishes to the retiree.*)

ON THE OCCASION OF AN ILLNESS

Leader: Dear friends, we have gathered together to pray for (*name*), who is ill. We are reminded that Jesus demonstrated great compassion toward the sick. Let us now hear the instruction given by James regarding prayer for the sick:

"Is anyone among you sick? Let him call for the elders of the church, and let them pray over him, anointing him with oil in the name of the Lord. And the prayer of faith will save the sick, and the Lord will raise him up" (5:14–15).

Let us pray.

Lord Jesus, we acknowledge Your power over sickness and all disease, which You demonstrated when You were among us. Give us hearts that are open to Your power. We pray in Your name. Amen.

The Scripture Readings

First Reader: A reading from the Old Testament:

"Now Naaman, commander of the army of the king of Syria, was a great and honorable man in the eyes of his master, because by him the LORD had given victory to Syria. He was also a mighty man of valor, but he was a leper. And the Syrians had gone out on raids, and had brought back captive a young girl from the land of Israel. She waited on Naaman's wife. . . . Then Naaman went with his horses and chariot, and he stood at the door of the house of Elisha. . . . And Elisha sent a messenger to him, saying, 'Go and wash in the Jordan seven times, and your flesh shall be restored to you, and you shall be clean.'. . . So he went down and dipped seven times in the Jordan, according to the saying of the man of God; and his flesh was restored like the flesh of a little child, and he was clean. Then he returned to the man of God, he and all his aides, and came and stood before him; and he said, 'Indeed, now I know that there is no God in all the earth, except in Israel'" (2 Kings 5:1–2, 9–10, 14–15).

This is the word of the Lord.

Response: Thanks be to God.

Second Reader: A reading from the gospel according to Mark: "Then He came to Bethsaida; and they brought a blind man to Him, and begged Him to touch him. So He took the blind man by the hand and led him out of the town. And when He had spit on his eyes and put His hands on him, He asked him if he saw anything. And he looked up and said, 'I see men like trees, walking.' Then He put His hands upon his eyes again and made him look up. And he was restored and saw everyone clearly" (8:22–25).

The Anointing and Prayer of Healing

(The elders of the church and/or members of the family may gather around the sick person. After placing oil on the forehead of the person in the name of the Father, the Son, and the Holy Spirit, place hands on the head, saying the following prayer:)

Leader: Let us pray.

307

O Lord, it is through Your power that Your
Son Jesus healed the sick and gave new hope.
Although we cannot presume upon Your will,
we do offer our prayer in faith for the healing
of (*name*). In Your will grant wholeness of
mind, body, and soul. Give peace and comfort
to both the sick and the well, that we all may
give glory to Your name, through Jesus Christ
our Lord. Amen.

(*As people depart, they may greet the sick person
with a Christian greeting, saying, "The Lord be
with you."*)

ON THE OCCASION OF DYING

(*In the absence of a pastor to comfort a person
who is dying, relatives and friends of the dying
may gather around the bed and read one or all of
the following Scriptures.*)

Psalm 23

"The Lord is my shepherd;
I shall not want.
He makes me to lie down in green pastures;
He leads me beside the still waters.
He restores my soul;

He leads me in the paths of righteousness
For His name's sake.
Yea, though I walk through the valley of the
    shadow of death,
I will fear no evil;
For You are with me;
Your rod and Your staff, they comfort me.
You prepare a table before me in the presence
    of my enemies;
You anoint my head with oil;
My cup runs over,
Surely goodness and mercy shall follow me
All the days of my life;
And I will dwell in the house of the LORD
Forever."

John 14:1–3

"Let not your heart be troubled; you believe in
God, believe also in Me. In My Father's house
are many mansions, if it were not so, I would
have told you; I go to prepare a place for you.
And if I go and prepare a place for you, I will
come again and receive you to Myself; that
where I am, there you may be also."

Revelation 22:1–5

"And he showed me a pure river of water of
life, clear as crystal, proceeding from the
throne of God and of the Lamb. In the middle
of its street, and on either side of the river,
was the tree of life, which bore twelve fruits,
each tree yielding its fruit every month. And

the leaves of the tree were for the healing of the nations. And there shall be no more curse, but the throne of God and of the Lamb shall be in it, and His servants shall serve Him. They shall see His face, and His name shall be on their foreheads. And there shall be no night there: They need no lamp nor light of the sun, for the Lord God gives them light. And they shall reign forever and ever."

Leader: Let us pray.

Lord, we commend your servant, (*name*), into Your tender love and care. Grant (*him/her*) the joy of Your kingdom and fill (*his/her*) life with everlasting peace; and bring us at that last day into the fellowship of our loved one. And may we live and reign together with You forever and ever.

Response: Amen.

ON THE OCCASION OF A DEATH

(*For a gathering after a funeral service.*)

Leader: Dear friends, we gather to mourn the death of (*name*), who has gone home to be with the Lord. Let us not mourn as those who have no hope; let us remember the word of the Lord:

"Death is swallowed up in victory./O Death, where is your sting?/O Hades, where is your victory?" (1 Cor. 15:54–55).

Let us pray.

Lord, God of life and death, we give You thanks for the life of (*name*), and for the joy we have had in knowing (*him/her*). Receive (*him/her*) into Your kingdom. Grant (*him/her*) rest and peace in You. Be present, O Lord, to those who remain. Grant us consolation and hope, and may we live for that day when we will be united with our loved ones and with You forever. Amen.

Reader: A reading from the gospel of John:
"Then Jesus said to them plainly, 'Lazarus is dead.'. . . So when Jesus came, He found that he had already been in the tomb four days. Now Bethany was near Jerusalem, about two miles away. And many of the Jews had joined the women around Martha and Mary, to comfort them concerning their brother. Then Martha, as soon as she heard that Jesus was coming, went and met Him, but Mary was sitting in the house. Then Martha said to Jesus, 'Lord, if You had been here, my brother would not have died. But even now I know that whatever You ask of God, God will give You.' Jesus said to her, 'Your brother will rise again.' Martha said to Him, 'I know that he will rise again in the resurrection at the last day.' Jesus said to her, 'I am the resurrection

and the life. He who believes in Me, though he may die, he shall live. And whoever lives and believes in Me shall never die. Do you believe this?' She said to Him, 'Yes, Lord, I believe that You are the Christ, the Son of God, who is come into the world'" (11:14, 17–27).

This is the word of the Lord.

Response: Thanks be to God.

The Prayer of Commitment

Leader: Let us commit our dear loved one to the Lord. Lord Jesus, You who suffered death on the cross, You who destroyed the power of death by Your wounds, You who rose victorious from the grave, You who ascended into the heavens, You who are seated at the right hand of the Father, receive (*name*) into the fellowship of Your kingdom. Grant that (*he/she*) may join with the cherubim and seraphim to sing the new song and bless Your holy name. In that place where there are no tears, nor death, nor sorrow, nor crying, nor pain, grant the joy of a new body and a new life for our loved one. And in that place where there is no more night, give to (*name*) the light of Your countenance. In the name of the Father and of the Son and of the Holy Spirit.

Response: Amen.

Leader: Our loved one lives. Be at peace!

ON THE OCCASION OF A HOUSE BLESSING

Leader: Dear friends, we gather in His name to give thanks for this house, to dedicate it and the people who live here to the service of Almighty God.

Hear the word of the Lord from the gospel of Matthew: "And when you go into a household, greet it. If the household is worthy, let your peace come upon it. But if it is not worthy, let your peace return to you" (10:12–13).

Let us pray.

Lord, we give thanks for this house and those who make it a home. May this be a place in which Your presence is known in thought, word, and deed. May the lives of those who live here be rich in joy, and may those who come under this roof be filled with gladness and peace, through Jesus Christ our Lord.

Response: Amen.

First Reader: A reading from the Old Testament:
"Lord, who may abide in Your tabernacle?
Who may dwell in Your holy hill?
He who walks uprightly,
    And works righteousness,
    And speaks the truth in his heart;

313

He who does not backbite with his tongue,
  Nor does evil to his neighbor,
  Nor does he take up a reproach against his
    friend;
In whose eyes a vile person is despised,
But honors those who fear the LORD;
He who swears to his own hurt and does not
    change;
He who does not put out his money at usury,
  Nor does he take a bribe against the
    innocent.
He who does these things shall never be
    moved" (Ps. 15).

This is the word of the Lord.

Response: Thanks be to God.

Second Reader: A reading from the gospel according to Saint John:
"In my Father's house are many mansions; if it were not so, I would have told you. I go to prepare a place for you. And if I go and prepare a place for you, I will come again and receive you to Myself; that where I am, there you may be also. And where I go you know, and the way you know. Thomas said to Him, 'Lord, we do not know where You are going, and how can we know the way?' Jesus said to him, 'I am the way, the truth, and the life. No one comes to the Father except through Me'" (14:2–6).

This is the word of the Lord.

Response: Thanks be to God.

(The following prayer may be said in each room or in one room representing the whole house.)

Leader: Let us pray.

Father, You who are the giver of every good and perfect gift, we acknowledge Your blessing in giving (*us/them*) this place to reside. Send Your Spirit into this house that it may be a place of good and not of evil, a place of peace and not of chaos. Grant that those who live here may be filled with Your Spirit. Cause that in this house the ministry of love and compassion may be experienced by all who come and go from this place. And grant us all Your eternal joy, through Jesus Christ our Lord. Amen.

ON THE OCCASION OF HAVING FRIENDS OVER

Leader: My dear friends, I bid you to participate with me in a custom centuries old. In the early days of the church, Christians surrounded their meal with prayer. Today we recall the ancient tradition of the *agape* feast and use the meal prayers handed down to us from the early church.

Prayer before the Meal

> (*Taking a piece of bread and holding it that all may see, pray:*)

Leader: We thank You our Father, for the life and knowledge You have revealed through Jesus, Your Child.

Response: Thanks be to God.

> (*Taking a cup filled with drink and holding it that all may see, pray:*)

Leader: We thank You, our Father, for the holy line of David, through which You have revealed Jesus, Your Child.

Response: Thanks be to God.

> (*You may pass the bread and drink to be eaten in celebration of creation and of God's good gifts, if you wish. The meal may be eaten.*)

Prayers after the Meal

Leader: Let us pray.

We thank You, holy Father, for Your sacred name, which You have lodged in our hearts, and for the knowledge of faith and immortality, which You have revealed through Jesus, Your Child. To You be glory forever. Almighty Master, You have created everything for the sake of Your name, and have given men food and drink to enjoy that they may thank You. But to us You have given spiritual food and drink and eternal life through Jesus, Your Child. Above all, we thank You that You are mighty. To You be glory forever. Remember, Lord, Your church. Save it from all evil, and make it perfect by Your love. Make it holy and gather it together from the four winds into Your kingdom, which You have made ready for it. For Yours is the power and glory forever.

Let grace come and let this world pass away.

Hosanna to the God of David.

Response: Amen.

The Kiss of Peace

Leader: The peace of the Lord be with you.

Response: And also with you.

> (*Exchange Christian greetings with a handshake or an appropriate embrace, saying, "The Peace of the Lord be with you."*)

THANKSGIVING DAY

Leader: Today is a special day in the life of our nation and in the life of our home. We gather together to give thanks to the Almighty for the blessings He has granted us and those whom we love.

Hymn: "Come, Ye Thankful People, Come"

Leader: Let us pray.

Father, we acknowledge Your goodness to us and to all humankind. Receive our words of praise to Your glory, and bless this food. May it strengthen our bodies and nourish our spirits. Keep us, Lord, mindful of the needs of others, through Jesus our Lord.

Response: Amen.

(*Here the meal may be eaten.*)

Readings and Prayers after the Meal

First Reader: A reading from the Old Testament:
"I will extol You, my God, O King;
And I will bless Your name forever and ever.
Every day I will bless You,
And I will praise Your name forever and ever.
Great is the Lord, and greatly to be praised;
And His greatness is unsearchable.

One generation shall praise Your works to another,
And shall declare Your mighty acts.
I will meditate on the glorious splendor of Your majesty,
And on Your wondrous works.
Men shall speak of the might of Your awesome acts,
And I will declare Your greatness.
They shall utter the memory of Your great goodness,
And shall sing of Your righteousness. . . .

My mouth shall speak the praise of the LORD,
And all flesh shall bless His holy name
Forever and ever" (Ps. 145:1–7, 21).

This is the word of the Lord.

Response: Thanks be to God.

Second Reader: A reading from Paul's letter to the Romans:
"Oh, the depth of the riches both of the wisdom and knowledge of God! How unsearchable are His judgments and His ways past finding out!
'For who has known the mind of the LORD?
Or who has become His counselor?'
'Or who has first given to Him
And it shall be repaid to him?'
For of Him and through Him and to Him are all things, to whom be glory forever. Amen" (11:33–36).

This is the word of the Lord.

Response: Thanks be to God.

The Prayer of Thanksgiving

Leader: Let us offer a prayer of thanksgiving to God for His blessings on us this past year. In the prayer I will pause so that you may be able to offer sentence prayers of thanksgiving from your own experience.

Let us pray.

Almighty God and Father, we most humbly offer You our prayers of praise and thanksgiving. We most especially thank You for the gifts and benefits of this past year. (*Here may be added personal prayers of the people.*) Help us, Lord, to be ever mindful of the needs of others, through Jesus Christ our Lord. Amen.

VALENTINE'S DAY

Leader: Dear family and friends, today we celebrate Valentine's Day, a day of love. Centuries ago a cleric, Valentine by name, was put to death for his faith in Christ. A church, built in his name, commemorated his sacrificial death; and a day was named in his honor. In the late medieval period, Valentine's Day was associated with the mating of the birds. This stimulated people to send love notes to each other. Today we want to celebrate love, not in a secular way, but as a gift of God, by remembering Saint Valentine, who out of love gave his life to God.

Let us pray.

Lord God, You who are love, whom we also love and serve, grant that we, like your servant Valentine, may love You even to our death if necessary. Cause our love today for spouse, relative, and friend to be strengthened in Your love, through Jesus Christ, to whom be glory forever. Amen.

The Scripture Reading

Reader: A reading from 1 Corinthians:
"Though I speak with the tongues of men and of angels, but have not love, I have become as sounding brass or a clanging cymbal. And though I have the gift of prophecy, and understand all mysteries and all knowledge, and though I have all faith, so that I could remove mountains, but have not love, I am nothing. And though I bestow all my goods to feed the poor, and though I give my body to be burned, but have not love, it profits me nothing. Love suffers long and is kind; love does not envy; love does not parade itself, is not puffed up; does not behave rudely, does not seek its own, is not provoked, thinks no evil; does not rejoice in iniquity, but rejoices in the truth; bears all things, believes all things, hopes all things, endures all things. Love never fails. But whether there are prophecies, they will fail; whether there are tongues, they will cease; whether there is knowledge, it will vanish away. For we know in part and we prophesy in part. But when that which is perfect has come, then that which is in part will be done away. When I was a child, I spoke as a child, I understood as a child, I thought as a child; but when I became a man, I put away childish things. For now we see in a mirror, dimly, but then face to face. Now I know in part, but then I shall know just as I also am known. And now abide

faith, hope, love, these three; but the greatest of these is love" (13).

This is the word of the Lord.

Response: Thanks be to God.

The Prayer Commitment

Leader: Let us pray.

Lord, receive this our thanks for the love You give us for Yourself and each other. Grant us an increase of love. May we love You more and more and may our love for each other increase daily. Fill us with joy and grant us Your peace, through Jesus Christ our Lord.

Response: Amen.

.MOTHER'S DAY.

Leader: Dear family, this day is a very special day for us all, for on this day we honor Mother. Hear the word of the Lord: "Honor your father and your mother, as the LORD your God has commanded you, that your days may be long, and that it may be well with you in the land which the LORD your God is giving you" (Deut. 5:16).

Let us pray.

Lord God of the universe, You who created

and brought forth all things, You have given
us mothers who like Yourself bring forth life.
Like You, our mother has nursed us, nurtured
and tenderly cared over us. Feeding and
clothing us, our mother has drawn us to her
side giving us her very life. Grant that we
should honor her and love her, to her benefit
and Your glory, through Christ. Amen.

The Scripture Readings

First
Reader: A reading from Proverbs:
(husband) "Who can find a virtuous wife?
For her worth is far above rubies.
The heart of her husband safely trusts her;
So he will have no lack of gain.
She does him good and not evil
All the days of her life. . . .
She extends her hand to the poor,
Yes, she reaches out her hands to the
needy. . . .
Strength and honor are her clothing;
She shall rejoice in time to come.
She opens her mouth with wisdom,
And on her tongue is the law of kindness.
She watches over the ways of her household,
And does not eat the bread of idleness.
Her children rise up and call her blessed;
Her husband also, and he praises her:
'Many daughters have done well,
But you excel them all.'
Charm is deceitful and beauty is vain,

But a woman who fears the LORD, she shall be
   praised.
Give her of the fruit of her hands,
And let her own works praise her in the gates"
   (Prov. 31:10–12, 20, 25–31).

This is the word of the Lord.

Response: Thanks be to God.

Second   A reading from Proverbs:
Reader: "My son, hear the instruction of your father,
And do not forsake the law of your mother;
For they will be graceful ornaments on your
   head,
And chains about your neck. . . .
Bind them continually upon your heart;
Tie them around your neck.
When you roam, they will lead you;
When you sleep, they will keep you;
And when you awake, they will speak with
   you.
For the commandment is a lamp,
And the law is light;
Reproofs of instruction are the way of life"
   (1:8–9; 6:21–23).

This is the word of the Lord.

Response: Thanks be to God.

The Blessing

Leader: Each of us will now bless Mother saying:
"What I like about you is————" or "I appreciate and acknowledge you for————."

Let us bless our mother in prayer. Lord God, You have given mothers to the world and blessed the fruit of their womb. You, Lord, are the Mother of Elizabeth, the mother of John, and of Mary, the mother of Jesus. Hear, O Lord, our prayer and bless the mother of this home. Grant her strength to fulfill her calling. May she be filled with joy and laughter. May she experience peace of mind and heart, and may her children rise up to bless her, through Jesus Christ our Lord.

All: Amen.

FATHER'S DAY

Leader: Dear family, this day is a very special day for us all, for on this day we honor Father. Hear the word of the Lord: "Honor your father and your mother, as the LORD your God has commanded you, that your days may be long, and that it may be well with you in the land which the LORD your God is giving you" (Deut. 5:16).

Let us pray.

Lord God, we gather in Your name to honor our father. Like You, our father provides for us, directs our paths into truth, and leads us into the way that is right. Grant that we

should love him to his benefit and Your glory,
through Christ our Lord. Amen.

The Scripture Readings

First
Reader: A reading from Proverbs:
  (wife) "Hear, my children, the instruction of a
              father,
And give attention to know understanding;
For I give you good doctrine:
Do not forsake my law.
When I was my father's [*son, daughter*],
Tender and the only one in the sight of my
      mother,
He also taught me, and said to me:
'Let your heart retain my words;
Keep my commands, and live.
Get wisdom! Get understanding!
Do not forget, nor turn away from the words
      of my mouth.
Do not forsake her, and she will preserve you;
Love her, and she will keep you.
Wisdom is the principal thing;
Therefore get wisdom.
And in all your getting, get understanding.
Exalt her, and she will promote you;
She will bring you honor, when you embrace
      her.
She will place on your head an ornament of
      grace;
A crown of glory she will deliver to you'"
      (Prov. 4:1–9).

This is the word of the Lord.

Response: Thanks be to God.

Second Reader: A reading from Proverbs:

"My son, do not forget my law,
But let your heart keep my commands;
For length of days and long life
And peace they will add to you.
Let not mercy and truth forsake you;
Bind them around your neck,
Write them on the tablet of your heart,
And so find favor and high esteem
In the sight of God and man.
Trust in the LORD with all your heart,
And lean not on your own understanding;
In all your ways acknowledge Him,
And He shall direct your paths.
Do not be wise in your own eyes;
Fear the LORD and depart from evil.
It will be health to your flesh,
And strength to your bones.
Honor the LORD with your possessions,
And with the firstfruits of all your increase;
So your barns will be filled with plenty,
And your vats will overflow with new wine.
My son, do not despise the chastening of the
        LORD,
Nor detest His correction;
For whom the LORD loves He corrects,
Just as a father the son in whom he delights"
        (3:1–12).

This is the word of the Lord.

Response: Thanks be to God.

The Blessing

Leader: I invite you to join with me in blessing Father by saying: "What I like about you is ———— ," or "I appreciate and acknowledge you for ————."

Let us bless our Father in prayer.

Father in heaven, we bless You for our father on earth. For You have given him to us to be a mirror of Your fatherly goodness. From him we have learned of Your love, through him we have experienced Your covenantal faithfulness, by his life we have a model of Your law, and from his sacrificial self-giving we have learned of Your sacrifice for us. Grant him fullness of life. May he enjoy strength and health. May he experience joy and laughter, and may his children rise up to make him glad. We pray this for his benefit and to the glory of God the Father in whose name we pray.

All: Amen.

APPENDIX I Dates of the Church Year

Year	First Sunday of Advent	Lent Begins with Ash Wednesday	Easter	Pentecost
1997	30 November	12 February	30 March	18 May
1998	29 November	25 February	12 April	31 May
1999	28 November	17 February	4 April	23 May
2000	3 December	8 March	23 April	11 June
2001	2 December	28 February	15 April	3 June
2002	1 December	13 February	31 March	19 May
2003	30 November	5 March	20 April	8 June
2004	28 November	25 February	11 April	30 May
2005	27 November	9 February	27 March	15 May
2006	3 December	1 March	16 April	4 June
2007	2 December	21 February	8 April	27 May
2008	30 November	6 February	23 March	11 May
2009	29 November	25 February	12 April	31 May
2010	28 November	17 February	4 April	23 May

APPENDIX II:
About the Advent Wreath

Growing up in a Baptist parsonage, I always loved and cherished the Christmas season. Now as an adult I've long since forgotten what I received on Christmas day. What still lingers in my memory, though, are the symbols of Christmas that filled our home with joy, laughter, and an increased sensitivity to the great festival. The memory of the family gathered around the manger scene, the brightly lighted tree, or the Christmas morning ritual of reading the birth account of Jesus (before opening presents) now fills me with nostalgia and recreates the meaning of celebrating Christmas with my family.

In the past two decades the ancient custom of the Advent Wreath has enjoyed an immense recovery throughout the world as a symbol that does for Advent what the manger scene and the Christmas tree do for Christmas. So widespread is this phenomenon that I have chosen to add an Appendix to introduce it to those who have only heard of it, and to explain how to use it as a meaningful way to prepare the family for Christmas.

While the specific origins of the Advent Wreath are not known, we do know that it began centuries ago in what is now Eastern Germany and was then associated with the Yule tradition of burning lights. By the sixteenth century these lights became Advent symbols in Christian homes. And from that tradition, the custom of a different candle light to represent each of the four weeks of Advent developed.

Originally the Advent Wreath was a wreath of evergreens placed in a circle containing four candles. Each Sunday a different candle was lighted until all four candles shed their light together. The gradual increase of light symbolized the growing anticipation of the birth of Jesus.

More recently the tradition of placing a fifth candle in the middle of the wreath has developed. This candle is usually double or more the size of the other candles, and is known as the Christ candle. It signifies the one around whom the anticipation builds, and is not lighted until the family celebrates the birth of Jesus.

While an already made Advent Wreath can be purchased at a Christian book store—or, as I have recently seen, are now available in many department stores—you may prefer to make your own. Make a circle as small or as large as you wish from coathangers or other sturdy wire. Then purchase a bunch of evergreens and attach them to the circle with fine wire. Finally, place the four Advent candles around the outer rim, and the Christ candle in the midst. Now you are ready to celebrate Advent.

You will note as you look at the family Advent celebrations that the family service of each week has a different emphasis. This emphasis is articulated throughout each family service in the prayers, Scripture readings, and dialogue. Each successive candle represents a movement one step closer to the realization of Jesus' birth:

First Week—Vigilant waiting for the birth of Christ;

Second Week—Personal preparation for the birth of Christ;

Third Week—The joy of our waiting;

Fourth Week—The Incarnation of the Word in the womb of the Virgin Mary;

Christmas Day—The Christ candle represents the birth.

Finally, by the colors of the candles you will want to symbolize the twin themes of Advent—preparation and joy. Since preparation is solemn and even penitential, the first, second, and fourth candles should be dark blue or purple. The third candle which symbolizes the joy of anticipation is always rose-colored. And the Christ candle is white, the symbol of festivity.

You can place the Advent Wreath on your dining table or hang it above, or place it in another central location. It enhances the Advent meals to have the wreath in a place visible to the entire family.